The Science
of
SHAME
And Its Treatment

"*The Science of Shame and Its Treatment* is a well-researched book that has many practical applications for clinicians who are working with patients who have experienced trauma, abuse, and neglect. It clearly distinguishes shame from guilt (a key concept), while it focuses on the etiology and treatment of shame. I plan to use this book as a guide in working with patients who have been burdened with incapacitating shame for most of their lives."

—**DAN S. FOGEL**, LMSW, CLINICAL SOCIAL WORKER, GRAND RAPIDS, MICHIGAN

T0150227

"*The Science of Shame and Its Treatment* is invaluable for anyone in a therapeutic process. Dr. Fishkin's in-depth discussion on shame begins by first defining and clarifying the difference between shame and guilt. That alone is worth the price of the book!"

—**A.D. BURKS** AUTHOR OF *SEX & SURRENDER: AN ADDICT'S JOURNEY* AND *THE 4 STEPS: A PRACTICAL GUIDE TO BREAKING THE ADDICTIVE CYCLE*

"*The Science of Shame and Its Treatment* is a detailed description of the nature of shame and brings clarity to this much maligned emotion. It is a must read for therapists who are helping their clients move from believing they are worthless to knowing they have inherent worth."

—**Pia Mellody,** SENIOR THERAPIST AT THE MEADOWS TREATMENT CENTER AND AUTHOR OF *FACING CODEPENDENCE: WHAT IT IS, WHERE IT COMES FROM, HOW IT SABOTAGES OUR LIVES*

"Dr. Fishkin breaks new ground in his book *The Science of Shame*, in which he explores a basic part of character development. The book's insights definitely helped me understand myself better."

—**HARRY SALTZGAVER,** EXECUTIVE EDITOR, GAZETTE NEWSPAPERS, LONG BEACH, CA

The Science
of
SHAME
And Its Treatment

Gerald Loren Fishkin, Ph.D.

Foreword by Rita Smilkstein, Ph.D.

Parkhurst Brothers Publishers

MARION, MICHIGAN

© Text copyright 2016 by Gerald Loren Fishkin, Ph.D. All rights reserved under the laws and treaties of the United States of America and all international copyright conventions and treaties. No part of this book may be reproduced in any form, except for brief passages quoted within news or blog features about the book, reviews, etc., without the express prior written consent of Permissions Director, Parkhurst Brothers Publishers, Inc.

www.parkhurstbrothers.com

Parkhurst Brothers books are distributed to the trade through the Chicago Distribution Center, and may be ordered through Ingram Book Company, Baker & Taylor, Follett Library Resources and other book industry wholesalers. To order from Chicago Distribution Center, phone 1-800-621-2736 or send a fax to 800-621-8476. Copies of this and other Parkhurst Brothers Inc., Publishers titles are available to organizations and corporations for purchase in quantity by contacting Special Sales Department at our home office location, listed on our web site. Manuscript submission guidelines for this publishing company are available at our web site.

Printed in the United States of America

2018 2019 2020   16 15 14 13 12 11 10 9 8 7 6 5 4 3 2

Library of Congress Cataloging-in-Publication Data

Names: Fishkin, Gerald Loren, author.
Title: The science of shame : and its treatment / Gerald Loren Fishkin ;
    foreword by Rita Smilkstein.
Description: First edition. | Marion, Michigan : Parkhurst Brothers
    Publishers Inc, 2016.
Identifiers: LCCN 2015049275 | ISBN 9781624910746 (paperback)
Subjects: LCSH: Shame. | BISAC: PSYCHOLOGY / Emotions. | PSYCHOLOGY /
    Clinical Psychology. | PSYCHOLOGY / Psychotherapy / Counseling.
Classification: LCC BF575.S45 F57 2016 | DDC 152.4/4--dc23
LC record available at http://lccn.loc.gov/2015049275

ISBN: Original Trade Paperback   978-1-62491-074-6
ISBN: e-book   978-1-62491-075-3

Parkhurst Brothers Publishers believes that the free and open exchange of ideas is essential for the maintenance of our freedoms. We support the First Amendment of the United States Constitution and encourage all citizens to study all sides of public policy questions, making up their own minds. Closed minds cost a society dearly.

Cover and interior design by   Linda D. Parkhurst, PhD
Proofread by   Bill and Barbara Paddack
Acquired for Parkhurst Brothers Inc., Publishers by :   Ted Parkhurst

All URLs in this book are being provided as a convenience and for informational purposes only; they do not constitute an endorsement or an approval by the publisher of any of the products, services or opinions. Parkhurst Brothers Publishers bears no responsibility for the accuracy, legality or content of linked sites or for that of subsequent links. Contact external sites for answers to questions regarding their content.
032016

Dedication

To Kathy and Cooper for your unconditional love and support.

ACKNOWLEDGEMENTS

The challenge of going from inspiration to final manuscript completion requires more than an author's sweat and toil—it takes individuals with dedication and skill to transform the author's vision into a readable and cohesive presentation. In that regard, I have been honored to work with an editorial team of the highest caliber.

My gratitude and appreciation to Pia Mellody and the clinical staff at The Meadows, Wickenburg, Arizona, for their groundbreaking work in the treatment of toxic shame and addiction and for their incalculable contribution to this book. It was through their work that I was inspired to ask the questions that resulted in this present work. For that, I offer my heartfelt appreciation and respect.

My love and gratitude go to Vinita Jha, my "editor in chief," who maintained my vision and voice from the inception of this project to its completion and whose insight, depth of caring, and deadline setting showed the love and dedication to this lengthy project that kept me constantly moving forward.

Kate Karp not only served as copy editor but also carried the editorial torch across the finish line. More than dotting the i's and crossing the t's, Kate sat with me through the critical cleanup process of manuscript completion with care, support, and validation that we were on the right track. It is such an honor to work with you. Kate Bandos of KSB Promotions and my publicist for many years, I cannot thank you and Doug enough for your care and expertise in helping me promote my vision to the world.

Ted Parkhurst, president of Parkhurst Brothers Publishers, I am honored and grateful for your trust, support and belief in my vision of shame and its healing, and for giving us a home from which to tell this story. You are my "ombudsman for the reader." Linda Parkhurst, book designer at Parkhurst Brothers, took my naked manuscript and clothed it well with a beautiful design, you have my deepest appreciation.

I have been blessed throughout my life to be part a loving and extremely brilliant and talented family. In that regard, I cannot express the depth of contribution to this book by Professor Rita Smilkstein, Ph.D., noted educator, author, and international lecturer and also my loving cousin. Rita not only took the time to read the final manuscript but also ripped it apart and put it back together again in a more readable and theoretically cohesive manner, and then honored me with a heartfelt foreword to this book. I owe her my deepest love and respect.

Finally, to all my patients over the past forty-five years, I offer you my deepest respect, appreciation, gratitude and love for trusting and allowing me into your world to share both your pain and your courage to change, without which this book could not have been written.

TABLE OF CONTENTS

ILLUSTRATIONS

FIGURES

TABLES

FOREWORD

I wish I'd had this book fifty years ago when I started teaching, first from grades seven through twelve, then at a two-year community college, and now at a university. There was one problem that kept breaking my heart over all the years and for which I had no solution: Why did some students who seemed capable and motivated start missing classes and not turn in their work on time or at all? I tried talking with them to understand why they seemed to be sabotaging themselves. No one could tell me. In fact, if I insisted on pursuing the issue, some of these students would drop out of my community college class—some would even drop out of school.

During a conversation with a young man one day after class, I asked him why he had stopped coming to class regularly, was not doing all his assignments, and had not shown up for the midterm exam. He just shook his head and started to leave. I asked him to sit down. I said that I wanted to talk with him because I knew he was a very intelligent person but seemed for some reason to be sabotaging himself. Again, he started to get up to leave. I said, "I know there's a reason, because you could be an excellent student." He shook his head and continued getting up. I knew there was an answer somewhere, and I cared about this young man. So I said as gently but as firmly as I could, "Please sit down. Now put your hands over your eyes." He sat down and put his hands over his eyes. Then I said, "Think back to when you were a child. Did anything ever happen then to make you want to fail and not succeed?" He shook his head vigorously and tried to stand up again. This time I said, "Wait. Put your hands over your eyes again and think back. Did anyone ever tell you not to succeed?" He sat there with his hands over his eyes, shaking his head. Then, he stopped shaking his head. A moment later, he began kicking his feet and punched out with one hand, the other one still over his eyes.

I cried out, "What are you remembering!" With both hands back over his eyes, he said, "When I was a kid, my dad always yelled at me, 'You think you're smarter than I am!' And he'd kick me and hit me!"

So that was the answer. He had been severely rejected and abused for being smart, so whenever he began to be successful at anything, he would feel his dad's fists and feet and would stop trying. Now that I understood, I was able to help him. We worked together, and with my support and encouragement, he began to succeed. A few years later, after graduating, he entered the university and had great success.

But why did this dynamic—his father's anger and punishment—have such a devastating effect on him? I didn't understand it and couldn't find any information about it—apparently no one had researched it or written about it—until I asked Dr. Fishkin. He said it sounded as if this student had been severely shamed by his father. He explained what shame is and told me he was writing a book about shame, its cause, and how to treat it based on his research about the brain and his successful experiences with many of his own patients.

I recently read his final working draft and was not only mesmerized—I was also enlightened! His book explains what shame is, what causes it, how to recognize it, how it's different from guilt, and how it can be successfully treated.

Every therapist and every teacher should read this book and use it to help shame-ridden patients and students.

Dr. Fishkin, thank you for this priceless gift, this true life-saver!

RITA SMILKSTEIN, PH.D.
WESTERN WASHINGTON UNIVERSITY
WOODRING COLLEGE OF EDUCATION

PREFACE

The year was 1962. Listening to the lectures in my first college psychology class, I was thoroughly impressed by what appeared to be a discipline rooted in theory—and lots of it—in every arena. From learning and behavior theories to perception, motivation, cognition, and emotion, psychology offered both an academic and a scientific approach to the human experience.

In his presentation on emotion, the psychology professor focused on the current theories about *affects*, our conscious observable feelings and reactions, as the foundation of our emotional states. Affects were said to be the subjective basis of all human emotions, separate from objective physical states in the body. We studied emotion as the cause or result of a person's behavior and learned about all the scientific theories behind the emotions themselves. Unfortunately, there was little in the way of empirical research at the time to support these theories. Many pieces of the puzzle were still missing.

At that time, Freud's psychoanalytic theory was out and the rational behaviorism movement was in. With the ideas of Albert Ellis and the development of cognitive behavioral theory (CBT) and its many psychotherapeutic techniques, we forgot about the importance and role of affects on human emotion. We have ignored how preverbal associations form and express themselves through each individual's unique personality and sense of self. The beauty of CBT was that it was theory-based and, most important, rooted in empirical research. A growing body of work was now also empirically demonstrating CBT's efficacy in treating many mental and mood disorders, including stress and depression.

Fast-forward fifty years. We had now begun to hypothesize that the long-ignored affects are actually the movers and shakers of everything we are. It turns out that affects are the very foundation of our *self*, the core of our being. Psychological studies are beginning to focus on affects as the root of emotional learning. As we examine the nature of affects, we are starting to see how early-life abuse and trauma influence us on a preverbal and precognitive level, even before our first childhood experience of guilt. Before the cognitive-associative reaction of guilt, which has been widely studied and recognized in psychological theory and treatment, a traumatized child experiences the markedly painful and much less understood emotion of *shame*, which is a powerful affect. In Chapter 5, "Definitions and Foundations of Affective Learning," I have attempted to define affective learning both from an intrapsychic and an empirical perspective.

As a clinician, I can now recall so many patients with reported histories of childhood abuse and trauma who could only go so far psychotherapeutically with cognitive behavioral therapy. Sadly, these people terminated treatment without a resolution to their grief and suffering and with overwhelming experiences of shame. At that time, my only clinical frame of reference was the humanistic-existential orientation and

cognitive-behavioral treatment model. I had no other concep-
tual structure within which I could treat these individuals. The
cognitive-behavioral model was so comfortable with regard
to the categorization and treatment of a wide range of human
issues—but it did not tap into the critical shame core. Cognitive behavior therapy (CBT) worked well for the modification of
the well-understood emotion of guilt but not the lesser-recog-
nized shame. I started wondering why—why can't the memories
of early-life abuse and trauma be changed, modified, or erased
through cognitive restructuring or other CBT techniques?

It was through my meeting and work with leaders at the
forefront of the theory and treatment of addictive disorders—
they included John Bradshaw, Claudia Black, and Pia Mellody—
that I began to understand, effectively, why my treatment with
certain individuals ended prematurely. I did not know until then
about shame and its relationship to early-life trauma, neglect,
and abuse. Within the therapeutic model I had always practiced,
I did not conceptualize what I now understand as concealed
shame and shame-based behavior.

In retrospect, I can see how, with most of these individuals, the foundations of the structure of shame were laid very
early in their lives. However, those suffering from early trauma,
abuse, or neglect could not identify with the shame; but their
internal voice, or self-talk, certainly would not let them forget
it. This critical, judgmental internal voice told these people what
they believed anyway: that they really weren't valued, that they
were "less than." As I began to understand shame and its many
component parts, I began to see it as a complex structure with

a foundation and many rooms: the structure of shame contains consciousness and bonding, along with both psychosocial and cognitive development. Self-talk may be viewed as the intrinsic binding agent among all of these.

As it will become clear that shame is in fact an affective response—a very powerful, preverbal, psychophysiological reaction that some neuroscientists believe is associated with basic neurological structures, operating from birth, that provide sensory awareness and reactivity. Thus, affects are hypothesized to be the very foundation of our emotional development.

Shame itself starts with shaming agents—identified as parents, caregivers, extended family, or anyone who intentionally or unintentionally inflicts trauma or abuse, or physically or emotionally abandons a child. These shaming agents put into play an incredible and seemingly insurmountable backdrop of self-defeating behavior in their victims. Think about it: When you can hear the voice of your abusers inside your own head, it shapes you and tortures you and won't let you go. It is a real and undeniable part of you, and this most difficult realization can finally open many new doors to healing.

While my own road to awareness has been a long and seemingly perpetual one, I now feel invigorated and excited at the prospect of sharing in the lives of my patients at a much deeper level, with a more profound understanding of the pain and suffering that brought them to me in the first place. It is the reason I wrote this book.

INTRODUCTION

Look around you. Everyone you see shares a deep and terrible secret that no one ever talks about. It is, in fact, one of the best-kept secrets of all time, as universal and natural as the air we breathe, and just as pervasive. No one is immune to it.

Look inside yourself. It's in there, too. We can't remember when it started or where it came from, but everything we know about ourselves comes from it. We listen to it instinctively, hold it close impetuously, and follow it without question every moment of our lives. The secret is our *inner voice*—the *self-talk*, the primal and silent internal communication that formed alongside our psyches, feeding us continuous messages that control our behavior. We hear it, but we can never see or feel or detect it in any other way. This brings us to the terrible part: our inner voice can be unkind. It can be degrading, derisive, and awful. It can tell us everything we don't want to hear, but, even though it can also sometimes be supportive and positive, we find ourselves unable to avoid its negative messages.

No one could ever be as cruel to us as we are to ourselves—not even close! We suffer at the hand of our very own consciousness at any moment if we are feeling identified, objectified, and labeled by something vague and beyond our control and understanding. The voice in our head can violate us, judge us, and assault us; telling us that we are not good enough, bright enough, successful enough, or worthy. Our minds and thoughts can be shaped by a constant flow of negative self-talk more than we can ever imagine. If this voice is the one that creates our reality and perceptions, we usually fail to even recognize it. We don't remember when or how it began; it has slipped so perfectly into the depths of our consciousness that it deftly escapes detection. It has become a silent and invisible part of us, a stealthy messenger holding unrivaled power.

Philosophers have thought about this inner self for centuries, referring to it as a *homunculus*, a miniature and preformed version of ourselves that we hold inside us. This feeds into the idea of self-talk making us who we are as individuals. Modern neuroscience conjectures about the existence of self-talk as a continuous narrative feature of the mind, but it provides no fundamental explanation of its origins. Scientists don't know where self-talk really lives. What they do know is that negative self-talk thrives on self-doubt, humiliation, and condemnation, making it inherently destructive. They also know that it can hijack us emotionally without warning, turning a once happy moment into a suddenly dark one. We are left stuck in our tracks, wondering why we are so helpless but afraid to share our internal turmoil with anyone. The irony of negative self-talk is that despite its universal presence, people think that no one else experiences or is affected by it.

Nothing ever seems to change our negative self-talk. Even if we learn about it and identify it and take steps to modify or quiet it, the self-defeating monster refuses to be mollified. It keeps on judging us without waiting for or needing our permission. Understanding the nature of this self-talk explains why.

Self-talk is formed from our earliest life experiences. It's rooted in the time we began to learn about our world and ourselves, when we formed the basis of our conscious mind and self. As infants, when we were completely dependent on those who cared for us, the messages of our parents or caregivers gave birth to our self-talk. As our caregivers taught us with their words, feelings, and behaviors, we developed our own thoughts and reactions, forming an unbreakable bond. This is how self-talk is built into our systems.

Self-talk starts at the beginning of our lives and is born from our earliest experiences. Because of its early onset, self-talk is attached to a very basic set of assumptions about who, how, and *what* we are. This form of self-communication is associated with primal processes within the brain. The primal part of our brain, the hypothalamus, perceives and assesses environmental signals. Within the hypothalamus is the limbic system, the seat of our emotions. This limbic system connects us to our animal nature and directs our instinctive behavior. Self-talk is a primal function. It forms and feeds our feelings about ourselves—the negative feelings that lead to behavior created and then triggered by shame and guilt.

Guilt is a common theme in psychology and psychiatry. Guilt is cerebral and cognitive. It triggers an adrenal reaction in people with normal brain function. When we realize that we did something wrong, the bad, blaming thoughts immediately set in. This realization of wrongdoing springs from our intellect. The whole time we are feeling guilty, we are focused on our action and why it was wrong. We are thinking and analyzing based on our brain's reaction and training. Guilt is a cognitive-associative reaction, a violation of our learned values.

Shame, on the other hand, is an organic biological response that is expressed as a visceral and not an intellectual reaction. Shame is an affective reaction. Shame is internally focused on our self, not on our actions. In their book *Facing Shame*, Fossum and Mason (1986) say, "While guilt is a painful feeling of regret and responsibility for one's actions, shame is a painful feeling about oneself as a person" (5). Guilt says, "I've *done* something wrong"; shame says, "There *is* something wrong with me." Guilt says, "I've *made* a mistake"; shame says, "I *am* the mistake." Guilt says, "What I *did* was not good"; shame says, "I *am* no good." Both reactions are unavoidably tied to each other. Guilt can, and often does, lead to feelings of shame. Guilt and its handmaiden, shame, can paralyze––or catalyze—one into action.

The concept of shame has not been widely studied in psychology or reviewed in psychological literature. Most, if not all, writing about shame has arisen out of the addiction-and-recovery-treatment world. Shame has been primarily viewed as the cause or result of addiction processes. But what if shame is not just a factor in mental diseases and conditions? What if it's much, much more? Is it actually a basic part of us? Could it be that shame can actually form our psyche, creating our very idea of self and even determining our behavior? How is this possible?

Negative self-talk, as discussed in this book, is essentially the talk of shame. Our inner voice dredges up the worst of our history and throws it back at us, constantly reinforcing the worst of who we think we are. Negative self-talk's internal focus on who we are, not what we do, sounds functionally similar to shame. What if the two are intrinsically and permanently related?

Shame has two discernible components and a corresponding cognitive association in the form of negative self-talk. Some individuals are more predisposed to the experience of *toxic shame* and shame attacks than are others. (For purposes of the present writing, the operational definition of toxic shame is addiction and the addictive processes, no matter what they may be, and the attendant mood issues associated with the addictions.)

As we shall see in Chapter 4, infants and children who experienced early-life abuse, neglect, trauma or abandonment appear as adults to be more shame prone and experience unrelenting negative self-talk than those not exposed to such experiences.

In my work, I have come to recognize certain empirical antecedents of negative self-talk as they relate to shame and shame-based behavior. By evaluating shame as a construct with biological, developmental, familial, and social aspects, we can begin to look at shame from an empirical perspective. We find from the study of toxic shame that its development is not linear; rather, toxic shame develops from the interaction of physical development and psychosocial experiences. This book is a new approach to examining the properties of shame and self-talk within the context of what I believe to be a cohesive model of their relationship to each other.

My aim is to provide readers with an understanding of the properties of shame as a cause of negative self-talk—and how to treat it. The primary goal is to help in the clinical treatment of shame-based self-talk and behavior and the affective states that accompany the experience of shame.

By exploring shame and self-talk in this new light and perspective, my hope is also to enable readers to gain a new and insightful understanding of themselves, their behavior, and the primal internal voice—the secret they share with everyone else in the world. Further, through this study of shame in the context of early-life trauma, it is my fundamental belief that we can gain a better understanding of the addictive, compulsive, and emotional disorders that frequently develop as a corresponding aspect of toxic shame.

CHAPTER 1
SHAME

The Nature and Properties of Shame

Shame is one of the least recognized and understood aspects of human behavior and emotional experience. Until recently, it has been mostly neglected as a topic of clinical exploration and discussion in psychological literature. Historically, shame and guilt have not had clear distinctions. Both have been called "moral emotions" that are key components of psychological disorders from depression and anxiety to bipolar illness and eating disorders (Tangney, 1995). There has been, however, a recent resurgence of interest in shame as a distinct, unique, and important emotion.

> Now the subject of much attention and debate, shame is suddenly everywhere in the literature and is seen by some as 'the master emotion,' the unseen regulator of our entire affective life. Current research identifies shame as an important element in aggression (including the violence of wife-beaters), in addictions, obsessions, narcissism, depression,

and numerous other psychiatric syndromes (Karen, 1992, 40).

Although the concept of shame was not widely studied for many years, the earliest writing about shame appears in psychoanalytic literature. Shame was first seen as a component of narcissism. As such, it was associated with the emotions of grandiose pride, guilt, self-blame, and self-esteem. The experience of shame was seen as the result of one's failure to live up to the narcissistic standards of the ego ideal. Even in this early literature, shame's negative nature and its sole focus on the self are apparent (Tomkins, 1963).

Most if not all current literature about shame has arisen out of the twelve-step addiction-and-recovery-treatment world, with shame as a cause or result of addiction processes. This approach to the concept of shame is an effort to understand how shame represents itself in behavior. Through the study of emotional experiences of shame in infancy, childhood, and adulthood, the literature focuses on how it affects our sense of self and self-worth.

Most theoretical and clinical models of shame hypothesize that the affective state of shame is aroused when we feel unworthy or bad about our self. When experiencing shame, we associate our behavior with who we are rather than what we do. Our actions are associated with guilt. If we think our behavior is caused by our own flaws, we perceive the behavior as difficult or impossible to change. This perception reinforces our fear or belief that we are unworthy of love and belonging. With shame, we condemn our self. Conversely, guilt is the feeling we experience if we have done something wrong, made a mistake, or transgressed our values and beliefs. With guilt, our behavior is generally focused on a specific act or event, not on who we are or our sense of self.

Shame is mysterious—and elusive by nature. Shame can cause a wide range of behaviors but escapes detection or understanding because we cannot see or touch or measure it. We can only experience it. As such, shame is not empirical and cannot be subject to scientific methods of examination, testing, or manipulation. The experience of shame is a state of being. Until recently, it has been a concept that defies empirical understanding of its etiological roots. This has made the scientific study of shame difficult.

Despite its elusive nature, shame is a universal experience. We impute the existence of shame, according to our own description, when the affect is triggered or activated within us. We experience shame to one degree or another when it is triggered by our own actions or within our social interactions. Someone saying or doing something to us can certainly trigger shame, as can something we do our self. In fact, the very word *shame* evokes an instant sense of unease, discomfort, and a need to withdraw and hide. It is that powerful! The experience of shame is often considered a private emotion that involves "self-evaluating the self," and it can have a wide-ranging impact on an individual and his or her relationships (Tangney and Dearing, 2002).

Shame can be experienced in other strong affective forms like mortification and humiliation. Depending on the situation, shame can also appear as despair and remorse as well as embarrassment and apathy. Shame has a wide range along the spectrum of human emotion. However, we are ill-equipped to confront this array of crippling emotions. The only major defense against the various forms of shame is the repression of thoughts or images that trigger it. But why is this? Why don't we have a good set of defenses against such a harmful force?

The Shame Attack and the Wound of Shame

When shame is activated, when it attacks us, it actually stops all our rational thought processes. It is difficult, if not impossible, to think positively about something—anything—when we are experiencing self-loathing and worthlessness. You might say that one is ashamed to feel shame! We just want to shrink and become invisible when this happens. Instead of bravely confronting an attack of shame, our response is often to quickly and quietly conceal it. Ironically, this attempt to hide shame actually develops an additional, reactionary shame response. We hide what we are ashamed of, and then we feel ashamed about hiding it—quite a vicious cycle! To complicate matters further, defensively denying shame will likely lead us to avoid situations or people without any understanding of our motivation to do so. We are now confused—and still ashamed.

A shame attack is like the bully within. Pia Mellody, a leader in the field of recovery from early-life wounding and shame existence, explains this experience: "A 'shame attack' is a sudden, profound, almost overwhelming sense of being worthless, inadequate, bad, stupid, or ugly (derogatory words about our self often come to us in the process of a shame attack)" (2003, 140).

> In a shame attack, you may feel as though your body is getting smaller. You may blush, want to disappear, run away, or crawl under your chair. It seems that everyone is looking at you. Feeling nauseated, dizzy, or spacey is also common. You might start talking in a tiny childlike voice. There is a tendency to "replay the scene" in your mind and let the shame feelings increase the next time through. In general, the experience of a shame attack is a dreadful sense of inadequacy (Mellody, 2003, 103).

When we experience a shame attack, we typically want to hide or disappear immediately. The pain is overwhelming: our sense of self and self-worth is at once reduced to an infantile experience of total invalidation, self-repudiation, and mortification. Nothing else in our lives makes us feel like this. This uniquely strong affective response or reaction can, and usually does, reduce us to our primordial state of helplessness and emotional isolation. Shame is powerful because it is primal.

In her model, Mellody refers to "carried shame," a sense of shame that is transferred from parents or caregivers to a child, who then carries this same sense of shame. Carried shame and its negative messages are seen as abusive, critically affecting the child's developing sense of self and self-worth. In essence, children carry the burden of their caregivers' abuse, dysfunction, and inadequacy—their sense of shame—and identify with it. Then, they in turn carry it forward. This cycle of family shame can be generational unless intervened upon.

Mellody's model, including her shame-reduction-treatment approach, is nonempirical and is only based upon her many years of treating patients with severe addictive disorders. Her belief is that codependency is a shame-based disorder that affects our sense of self, one that is derived from our early-life experiences with our caregivers. John Bradshaw (1988) and many other therapists who write about addictions agree. Since all children are naturally fallible and imperfect and, therefore, vulnerable, shame is seen as a result of assaults on a child's sense of belonging and adequacy. Because children are defenseless and dependent, they fear alienation or abandonment. They fear that their physical and emotional needs won't be met if the people taking care of them see them as "bad." This fear is strong enough to allow manipulation and control by abusive others, creating the cycle of shame.

In his detailed historical essay on the nature of shame, psychologist Robert Karen writes,

> Shame of this sort can be understood as a wound in the self. It is frequently instilled at a delicate age, as a result of the internalization of a contemptuous voice, usually parental. Rebukes, warnings, teasing, ridicule, ostracism, and other forms of neglect or abuse can all play a part.... Nothing, apparently, defends against the internal ravages of shame more than the security gained from parental love, especially the sort of sensitive love that sees and appreciates the child for what he or she is and is respectful of the child's feelings, differences, and peculiarities.... Nothing seems to make shame cut more deeply than the lack of that love (1992, 43).

If the fragile, developing sense of self in children becomes wounded through assaults such as trauma, neglect, abandonment, and physical, mental and verbal abuse, children in such cases internalize the parent's abusive voice and negative judgments. They start to believe that they are worthless and less than what they should be. These children adopt the early messages of their parents, who are their first teachers and guides. *The way we speak and behave toward children becomes their inner voice.* Children in these situations actually learn to assertively inhibit themselves and restrict the expression of feelings like anger or aggression because they fear their internalized parents will cause them to feel shame. Thus, shame binds and limits our ability to fully experience, express, and represent our self. It's like a virtual straitjacket.

This inhibiting process erodes our sense of self-worth and invalidates our own needs. Along with developing negative self-judgments as carryovers from our earliest exposure to and experience with negative feedback, we also develop narrow pathways or parameters within which we learn to navigate our world in order to feel safe. An aspect of this early exposure to trauma or abuse is the development of imperative "shoulds" and "should-nots." It is through this inhibiting process that our sense of self-worth is further eroded and our emotional needs invalidated.

Children raised with excessive fear of negative feedback and a lack of emotional support often feel responsible for the things and events that were never in their control. They constantly feel that they "should have" or "shouldn't have" done a number of things and that this means something is wrong with them. This is the message inculcated by their caregivers, and it sticks like nothing else. A tragically misplaced blame has been transferred to the children by the adults, who were actually the ones responsible. This pathological sense of responsibility is not situational; it doesn't change based on one's circumstances or environment. It becomes a generalized, internalized belief that affects a person's entire sense of self-worth and self-image, leading to more fear of rejection. The alleged noncompliance with the seeming "shoulds" and "should-nots" affects everything the person thinks and knows about himself or herself. And it all starts with the childhood experience of shame, which has previously been ignored by counselors, clinicians, and therapists.

The shadow of shame is born and developed out of the helplessness of infancy and the innocence of childhood. A hallmark of childhood is a charming spontaneity, the pushing forward with whatever the heart desires without worry over the consequences. However, children who have been abused, demeaned, or traumatized in any way live in a much darker world. They actively inhibit their natural spontaneity over and over again out of fear of rejection or abandonment. Shame has cast its shadow over that person's life, changing it completely and refusing to leave.

The childhood fear of rejection and abandonment and its accompanying self-blame are, as we shall see, the most frequent cause of alcoholism, drug abuse, and general chemical dependency in adulthood. Addictions are often seen as a means of coping with the painful experiences of early-life abuse that we bury within our self in an attempt to hide them. Many adults raised in unhealthy environments either succumb to their self-defeating beliefs and negative self-judgments or develop overcompensating behaviors and psychological defenses as a way of dealing with their own demeaning internal voice.

Despite the theoretical model of shame and how we try to understand it, most clinicians who write about shame agree that it is almost always expressed through a physical event or feeling. This affect is most likely based on our early experiences, which reinforce our sense of vulnerability and disadvantage, of being "one down" or "less than." Rational thoughts, we've learned, are not present when we experience our shame. It is important to understand that our thoughts follow our experience of shame rather than the other way around. Shame is unlike guilt in this way. Thoughts or cognition precedes the experience of guilt, but not shame. Since shame is built into our systems and self-image, we experience it first and then think about it later. This makes us particularly exposed and susceptible to shame.

Thoughts associated with shame and negative self-talk are considered to be coterminous; that is, shame and negative self-talk are so linked that they are created and terminated together. Negative self-talk is primarily and essentially the talk of shame. Negative self-talk is what we hear when we are having a shame attack. The experience of shame calls up our first sense of help-lessness, a residuum of early-life abuse. We cannot seem to stop this powerful internal voice. "Negative self-talk is something that is not usually under our conscious control; it just happens by itself, and most people find it impossible to stop it or not do it" (Andreas, 2012, 1).

Shame is more than a feeling. Disconcerting feelings trigger painful thoughts, usually all too familiar thoughts that increase the shamed person's troubles. These thoughts [or self-talk] confirm the shamed person's belief of having something to feel ashamed about.... We do think about shame, and sometimes we cannot stop thinking about our embarrassments, defeats, and humiliations. We end up calling our self terrible names ("Dummy," "Idiot," "Bitch," et cetera). Self-hatred develops in this manner, one insult at a time (Potter-Efron & Potter-Efron, 1989, 13).

Anger, Rage, and Shame

Within the matrix of today's family system, shame is seen as a primary element associated with violence and aggression. This is especially true in cases of spousal and child abuse, addictions, narcissism, depression, and obsessive-compulsive disorders. In obsessive-compulsive disorders, the pathological need for perfection may be seen as overcompensation for an individual's deep-rooted sense of helplessness associated with shame and perceived imperfectness.

In our culture, for example, men are taught at an early age to be strong, confident, and unemotional. To be a "man" is to be impervious to anxiety, stress, uncertainty, and doubt. Most male children in our culture, however, are raised by females. The male image is largely a stereotype of how we should be rather than how we fundamentally are. Men have the capacity to feel or experience most, if not all, of the emotions women do, whether they feel comfortable expressing them or do not.

Parents, and especially fathers, typically deny or overcompensate for feelings of low self-worth or self-esteem. If not dealt with, patterns of shame-based behavior can be handed down from one generation to another.

> If a father was rejected by his own dad and experiences being defective as a result, he will very likely and unconsciously behave in ways toward his son that repeat the pattern. Even if nothing overt is done, the father's sense of shame itself may transfer. If a mother felt unwanted by her parents, she may subtly prohibit her son from getting close to her father; this interference induces shame in the son and thereby reenacts the drama. In such ways, shame is recycled and passed on from generation to generation (Kaufman, 1974, 573–574).

Thoughts associated with a sense of inadequacy, self-doubt, fearfulness, or neediness can trigger shame attacks that call up a primitive fear of abandonment, especially if we believe others can see who we really are. Often, men react to these feelings with rage instead of just anger. "Rage is different from anger. Rage protects the self against further exposure and further experiences of shame by both insulating the self and actively keeping others away. A pattern of escalating rage can result, with each participant blaming the other as a way of protecting himself against exposure" (Kaufman, 1974, 571).

Shame and its resulting anger and rage are not limited to our culture or gender. They are universal experiences. All children are helpless and vulnerable. All children have basic needs that are preverbal. All children fear abandonment at some level, especially children who are raised in an abusive, rigid, chaotic, or loveless environment. Whether you are a man, a woman, or a child, and no matter where you live and what you believe, you are vulnerable to the potentially devastating effects of shame.

When and How Shame Begins

The final factor completing the present model of shame is the approximate age and developmental stage at which the child first experiences shame.

Many early writers discussing shame believed that shame is part of the formulation of personality development and the child's differentiation from the mother or caregiver. During this process of differentiation, children begin to develop a sense of consciousness and core self, of who they are as differentiated from their environment and those who nurtured them (Damasio, 1999). The infant's brain is also developing during this process. As the brain's neurons multiply and synapses increase, the infant is beginning to formulate words. We know that infant language begins in the first half of the second year of life, as does the infant's sense of self.

Although work in the area of neuroscience and the empirical study of emotions is relatively new, we are beginning to develop a positive understanding of the biological basis of affect and affective learning. As summarized by Antonio Damasio, a pioneer and leader in the neuroscience of consciousness and identity regarding the development of emotion, "it is clear that several 'secondary' emotions begin to appear later in the human development, probably only after a concept of self begins to mature. Shame and guilt are examples of this later development; newborns have no shame and no guilt, but two-year-olds do. That does not mean, however, that secondary emotions are not biologically preset, in part or mostly" (Damasio, 1999, 342).

Affective states such as anger, fear, sadness, and joy show up in the brain as different patterns of blood flow, providing one possible explanation for how affect influences brain activity (Lane, et al. 1997; Bechara et al., 2000).

Picard et al. (2004) summarize the research on the relationship between affective learning and cognition:

> On the most fundamental level, an accelerated flow of findings in neuroscience, psychology, and cognitive science itself present affect as completely intertwined with thinking and performing important functions with respect to guiding rational behavior, memory retrieval, decision-making, creativity, and more. While it has always been understood that too much emotion is bad for rational thinking, recent findings suggest that so is too little emotion as well: when basic mechanisms of emotion are missing in the brain, then intelligent functioning is hindered. These findings point to new advances in understanding the human brain not as a purely cognitive information-processing system, but as a system in which the affective functions and cognitive ones are inextricably integrated with one another (253).

Erikson and the Theoretical Underpinnings of Shame

We have looked at shame from the aspect of early shame theory and the ontological experience of shame or the many ways in which we experience it. I have also cited studies validating the neurological substrates of affect and the universality of shame.

In general, the literature regarding shame and the development of shame is sparse. "Most writers have assumed until recently that shame could not exist until a child began to develop a distinct sense of self. Someone can only feel judged by others if he realizes others are separate from him. A child would not fear abandonment unless he knew it were possible to be abandoned" (Potter-Efron and Potter-Efron, 1989, 67).

No model of shame has been as widely adopted and discussed as that of Erik Erikson. Erikson was a German psychoanalyst who was heavily influenced by Sigmund Freud. Rather than adopting Freud's psychosexual theory of development, Erikson's model is based on a psychosocial progression of the way in which children develop into adulthood and the challenges faced in this process.

Erikson claimed that the individual simultaneously develops on three levels: biological, social, and psychological (Erikson, 1950, 1958, 1964, 1968). All children are born with certain basic tendencies and dispositions. What happens during the process of bonding and interaction with parents and caregivers provides the foundation of self-worth.

Erikson believed that around the second year of life, children struggle for autonomy through the process of differentiation, desperately wanting their own way. This period of development, called the Stage of Autonomy vs. Shame (as exemplified by its nickname, the "terrible twos"), demonstrates children's need for separation as well as for independence with their own mind and personality. It is interesting to note that this is the same period in which expressive language begins to develop; children at this developmental stage are able to express shame through the beginnings of negative self-talk.

During this stage, children are exploring their world, gaining independence and learning to do things for themselves. At this point, they have an opportunity to build self-esteem and autonomy as they learn new skills and start differentiating right from wrong. Children who are well cared for tend to have more self-assurance and consider themselves with pride, not shame. Children are highly vulnerable during this stage, sometimes also feeling shame and low self-esteem, especially if there is an inability to learn new skills.

According to Erikson, a child who is encouraged to try new things and is praised for successes will develop a strong sense of autonomy and positive self-esteem. A child who is discouraged from attempting new things—or yelled at, ridiculed, or subjected to other abuse—will develop a sense of shame and low self-esteem. If children are criticized, over-controlled, or not given the opportunity to assert themselves, they begin to feel inadequate and then doubt their ability to ever succeed or even survive. This sense of insecurity may also lead to overdependence on others.

Children at this age express a lot of "noes" as part of the active process of differentiation and self-identity, but they are also completely dependent upon parents or caregivers to provide for their every need. How that care is provided and how it is received may be seen as the foundation of self-identity and personality.

As we will see throughout this book, if children are abused, abandoned, neglected, or in any way prevented from enjoying a healthy, nontraumatic environment and normal developmental progression, they will experience, to a greater or lesser degree, shame and the manifestation of shame-based behaviors.

Although shame and affective triggers may appear difficult to understand and seemingly impossible to control, they're definitely not something to ignore. Their repercussions are too widespread, strong, and dangerous. Shame is permanent in nature, as its effects can be. The pain of shame can lead to feelings of severe hopelessness and depression. In the worst cases, shame can even result in suicide: the ultimate attack against the self. In following chapters, we will learn how to attack and conquer the pain of shame and begin to heal our patients' childhood wounds and a lifetime of negative self-talk. Fortunately, healing is possible.

Colleen's Story

Colleen was a thirty-five-year-old Caucasian female who had been a hairstylist for sixteen years. After suffering a seizure at work, she was referred by her primary-care physician for psychological evaluation and treatment.

Colleen presented with the following issues:

- She admitted to consuming half a fifth of whiskey every night. She stated that she had been doing this for the past five or six years.

- She suffered attacks of panic and anxiety and stated that they were getting worse.

- She said that she believed that she had obsessive-compulsive disorder (OCD) and that her anxiety was making the condition worse, especially her checking behaviors, which were often paralyzing.

- She described how sometimes before leaving for work, she took a half-hour to check everything in her home—sometimes twice—especially the stove, the oven, and all the operable windows.

- She stated that she was burned out on hairdressing and wanted to find another less-demanding career. She also described certain clients as being overly demanding.

- She didn't socialize. She spent much of her off-work time at home alone.

- She wanted to go back to school to complete her bachelor's degree, focusing on history.

Colleen's history revealed that her parents divorced when she was seven years old. Her mother had primary physical and legal custody. Because her mother worked, Colleen was the classic latchkey child.

As a youngster, Colleen was fearful and self-conscious. An only child, she had night terrors and always felt isolated and alone. She had poor socialization and felt "less than" other children, or not as important or worthy. She never recalled her mother praising her or giving her any attention when she came home from work; in fact, she remembered her mother as being "emotionally cold." She also believed that her mother resented her not only for the divorce but for being born.

Her mother parentified her by placing her in the middle of the divorce itself, speaking badly of Colleen's father and asking her for emotional support, which Colleen was not equipped to provide at her age. The more her mother leaned on her, the more anxious Colleen became and the more turbulent her gastrointestinal disorders were. Colleen recalled that from childhood to adulthood, she had always had problems eating and keeping weight on, attributing it to a "nervous stomach." At five feet eight inches tall, Colleen weighed only 102 pounds at the time treatment began.

As an adult, Colleen had experienced two horrifying traumatic experiences. The first occurred in August 1999 when Colleen was sixteen and went to visit her father at his apartment. She knocked on the door and heard no answer. It wasn't customary for Colleen's father to not answer his door, so she tried the knob and found that the door was unlocked. She walked in and found her father lying dead on the living room floor in a pool of blood. It turned out that he had been shot to death by a neighbor's son in a drug-related robbery attempt.

Six years before entering therapy, the second deeply disturbing event happened. Colleen and her best friend and work associate, Jana, went to get a drink one night after a fashion show. Upon leaving the venue, Jana ran across the street to get her car. One of her heels caught the median divider, and she tripped over it into oncoming traffic and was hit and run over by a truck. "One minute we were laughing and having fun, and the next minute I'm watching and I'm seeing her brains all over the road," Colleen tearfully recalled. "I was never equipped to deal with stress, crisis, or trauma; and that's all my life seems to be at this point."

Colleen revealed that she had never grieved for her father or Jana and instead drank to cover her feelings. She was frightened of feeling those emotions and felt shame about her life and what she was doing with and to it.

Since Colleen was an only child, she didn't have anyone to confide in about the trauma and tragedies that she had experienced. Although her mother was a successful insurance broker, Colleen said she was cold and distant. She felt that she never had bonded with her and never felt safe revealing her emotions to her mother.

Colleen described herself in the present as "a huge pessimist" and stated that she never said what was on her mind. She also said that she never talked about herself, especially in a positive way, and did not handle compliments well. "I don't trust what most people say, and I overanalyze and nitpick everything," she said. "I guess I'm just avoidant that way."

Regarding her alcohol and drug use, Colleen stated, "Obviously, I have a huge drinking problem. My pessimism sometimes overwhelms me." She further revealed that she always drank alone and never for any reason other than to self-medicate.

As for the present, Colleen said that she has no trust in either herself or others. She reported that up until six years ago, around the time of Jana's death, she felt confident about her work as a cosmetologist. Now, however, she said that she gets so anxious before doing certain procedures that she winds up "freaking myself out and placing myself in an acute anxiety state." She said that she hates doing hair coloring in particular, as she constantly assumes that the client won't like it.

Before beginning outpatient treatment, Colleen had entered a thirty-day detoxification treatment program for poly-substance abuse and clinical depression. The outpatient therapy initially focused on helping her to effectively deal with the post-traumatic stress effects of both her father's and Jana's tragic deaths. For the first time, Colleen had to confront her feelings in a way foreign to her. In the course of treatment, she was able to confront her mother within the safety of the clinical environment and revealed much, if not all, of what she had kept inside.

During group treatment, Colleen was able to reveal her uncompromising toxic self-talk and shame for the first time. It was during this process that she was able to see the relationship between her *anxious, negative inner voice* and her diminished creativity both as a stylist and how she lives her personal life. As Colleen reported, "I spent so much time trying to control my anxiety that I was always overwhelmed and exhausted."

Recognizing that her workplace had become a toxic environment for her, Colleen left her salon to become a full-time student, fulfilling her dream to pursue a degree in history.

CHAPTER 2

MIND, CONSCIOUSNESS, AND THE SEEDS OF SELF-TALK

Reflecting on Reflection

When you look in the mirror, what do you see? Yourself, of course, but is it really *you*? The image in the mirror is just a momentary reflection. As we all grow and develop, we learn to expect and recognize this reflection of our self in the mirror.

Does this temporary vision truly show us as individuals, and can we perceive therein all the myriad life experiences that take us up to the moment of reflection? Are we happy or sad at this moment? Do we feel anything? Are our inner states reflected in this single gaze? Can they even be reflected—or only felt? And when we look in the mirror, we may be conscious—but are we aware? Is consciousness the same as awareness? And what about the things we tell our self? Is self-talk the same as thinking?

What we see in the mirror is only an approximation of our self. It's only an image, one snapshot in time and space.

Understanding this reflection requires us to look deeper. To the outer world, our self is revealed through our actions and inter-actions. But our self is revealed to us only through introspective self-consciousness.

Mind and Consciousness

For centuries, we have attempted to understand the mind and consciousness. Philosophers from Aristotle to Daniel Dennett have postulated theories to account for processes of thinking and perceiving. The mind has been described function-ally as intellect, reason, perception, and will; it's been likened to "a computer.... [but] with a trillion moving parts" (Dennett, 2013).

Consciousness has been defined as awareness or, in cogni-tive terms, a part of the brain's information-processing center. There are certain aspects of mind and consciousness on which the disciplines of philosophy, psychology, and neuroscience appear to agree. These elements include the following:

- We never think about consciousness—we take it for granted.

- Physical phenomena and brain regions alone cannot explain consciousness.

- Being conscious is being aware.

- Consciousness is being known and knowing.

- Consciousness is self-reflecting mental life.

- Consciousness is the precondition for experiencing thought.

- Consciousness provides the foundation for perception, primarily spatial-temporal activity: the experience of time and space.

The Mind

The mind is not a perceptible object. It is not just the brain as a whole or its structural parts but much more than that.

The mind provides for the experience of conscious awareness. Consciousness is the precondition for awareness to take place: the awareness of self, of others, and of the environment. The state of consciousness includes all visual, auditory, and tactile experiences. Primary to the state of consciousness is consciousness of self. This state develops and grows over time. Infants have consciousness but no basis for personalizing their environment. This personalization occurs through the processes of human development and assigning meaning to experience, which an infant is incapable of doing.

The primary experience of what we call "mind" is thought. All thought involves plans, purposes, decisions, and judgments. Thought is typically associated with an intentional object, which may or may not match up to reality as we see it. Mental activity is always about something. Mental activity involves experiences and thoughts. The philosopher David Hume believed that our idea of reality is rooted in our experiences. From the standpoint of self-talk and self-judgment, the sense of self can be said to be rooted in all our experiences—especially those of our early life, including as foundation our primordial sensory experiences.

All children are born with certain basic tendencies and

dispositions. What happens during the process of bonding and interaction with parents and caregivers, however, also provides the foundation of an individual's self-worth.

As we shall see in the following chapter, bonding and attachment issues—and in the worst case, poor and absent associations—result in reactive attachment disorders (border-line personality disorder, borderline behavior, depression, and low self-esteem/self-worth-associated disorders of personality). Absent or poorly developed internal supports cause a failure in a child's ability to self-nourish and self-protect, and they can develop into compulsive disorders (drug addiction, alcohol abuse, and escape behavior).

The range of one's affective states or repertoire of emotional responses may be a direct function of attachment. Healthy attach-ment leads to a broad affective range, whereas poor or unhealthy attachment (reactive attachment disorder, or RAD) results in a limited, constricted range of the affective-cognitive potential. Harry Harlow's early research in the 1950s identified the rela-tionship of attachment to later development of emotional and social behavior. Warm, nurturing mothering resulted in healthy emotional and social behavior; and cold, detached mothering was associated with disorders of emotion and poor socialization. Borderline personality has also been found to be positively asso-ciated with reactive attachment disorder (Harlow, 1958).

Through healthy attachment, the infant learns the idea of a "safe me" and feels secure. Conversely, in poor bonding or attachment, the infant learns through affective association about the "bad me" or the "unsafe me." This sets the infant up for feelings of shame.

In their book *Letting Go of Shame*, Ronald and Patricia Potter-Efron support the belief that shame is inherent in the child's struggle for independence:

> Children start their lives feeling they are at the center of the universe. They have little understanding of boundaries between them and others. Only gradually do they realize that other people, especially their parents, lead separate lives in different bodies. The child who knows this also recognizes on some level that he could be abandoned by these people. The fear of abandonment is considered by many to be the core of shame. The shamed person feels he will be abandoned because he is not good enough to keep.

> The child struggles for reassurance that she will not be abandoned by demanding constant attention. But no parents can always stop whatever they are doing to watch or praise their children. All children will occasionally feel frustrated when they cannot be the center of attention. This is normal. It even helps a child realize she is simply human. She learns slowly that she is important enough to get attention from others some, but not all, of the time.

> When a child gets much too little attention, however, the outcome can also be negative. The child who is ignored too much can conclude that he is not worth any of his parents' time. Since the parents are the center of a child's universe, he may decide that nobody actually cares for him and no one is really interested in his existence. This child concludes that he must be "nothing."

When a child receives excessive parental rejection, it can devastate her, filling her with shame and driving her away from others. A child who receives disapproval messages too often may decide that there must be something very wrong with her (Potter-Efron and Potter-Efron, 1989, 68–69).

The Self

The notion of *self* has been the subject of philosophical question and debate for centuries. The questions of "Who am I?" "Why am I?" and "What motivates me?" all appear to revolve around the central question, "What comprises the self?" To this end, William James (1890) proffered a simple taxonomic scheme. He proposed two possible orders of self: an empirical self (the Me) and a knowing self (the I). The empirical Me is composed of three subsidiary types: the material self (the body), the social self (recognition from others), and the spiritual self (inner being).

James's conceptualization of self held for many years and typified the psychological thinking of the time, which was more descriptive in nature but lacked an empirical or a scientific foundation. In comparison, the behaviorism movement and its adherents took a strictly empirical approach to the study of behavior and abolished the notion of self as necessary to understand behavior. In this movement, thinking was relegated to only the operations that caused thinking to occur. What was thought about was not seen as significant to the study of behavior.

This extreme view of behavior led many psychologists at

the time to oppose its narrow perspective of human functioning. At the opposite end of the behaviorism movement was Gordon Allport (1955), one of the first American psychologists to focus on the study of the personality and often referred to as one of the founding figures of personality psychology.

Allport provided a generalized definition of self in terms of a process that unifies the personality and maintains its integrity. According to Allport, personality is made up of "habits and skills, frames of reference, matters of fact, and cultural values that seldom or never seem warm and important. But personality includes what is warm and important also—all the regions of our life that we regard as peculiarly ours" (1955, 40).

Although we can see that there is no unified definition of self, there appears to be agreement that self is founded neurologically through consciousness, awareness, and memory functions. Additionally, early-life trauma and abuse have a direct correlation with one's level of shame and critical self-talk. Nicolosi (2009) adds further support to the fact that how parents and caregivers treat a child directly affects that child's sense of safety and trauma-based fear reactions.

> When parents have failed to accurately mirror the small child's internal experience, and to model the lesson that feelings and expressing feelings are safe, he will be affectively disorganized and emotionally isolated. The child grows up learning to distrust his interior perceptions, and becomes prone to shame-infused shutdowns of emotional relations. His defenses will cause him to shift his attention back and forth from content to feelings, and then back again to content, but avoiding the link between the two. (Nicolosi, 2009)

Neuroscience and the Study of Self

To date, neuroscientists have been unable to explain why we have a subjective experience of self. While we have knowledge of the primary neural pathways and mechanisms that allow for consciousness to occur, we have no good explanation of how we become our own unique self.

However, in the same way that we do not have to know how an engine works in order to drive a car, it is unimportant to know the mechanisms of conscious experience. Instead, what is important is to understand how consciousness is affected by experience, how consciousness functions, and how therapy can help to modify shame associations and responses.

We might say that our sense of self is formed by our objective and subjective experiences. Further, our subjective experiences—portrayed through our conscious state—involve three basic functions:

- **Awareness**: A person can be conscious but not aware. An example is a vegetative state in which cerebral dysfunction causes a lack of response in a conscious patient.

- **Attention**: Attention is the cognitive and behavioral process of selectively concentrating on one aspect of the internal or external environment—such as our breath or a sound—while ignoring other things.

- **Self-Reference**: This is our relationship with our self vis–à–vis the external world. Self-reference involves our identity and is the area where shame and critical self-talk live.

Thus, consciousness is a subjective experience of a

something that is happening to a Me. We shall refer to the Me as the self.

In an attempt to add empirical understanding to the concept of self, Antonio Damasio (2010), one of the most prominent neuroscientists of our time, distinguishes three different aspects of self that we possess:

- **Proto-Self**: This is the interconnected and temporarily coherent collection of neural patterns representing the state of the organism moment by moment at multiple levels of the brain. The proto-self is unconscious or precognitive and may be seen as an accumulation of early-brain affective signatures, and, for our purposes, the affective signatures of very early-life trauma and abuse.

- **Core Self**: The core self does not change much throughout our lifetime. We are, however, conscious of the core self. Thus, we can speak of core consciousness, which is connected to our sense of self. For example, when in deep meditation or performing a mindless task such as picking weeds, we have a temporary absence of self.

- **Autobiographical Self**: This aspect of our self is based on memory as well as anticipations of the future. Our autobiographical self grows throughout our lifetime. Loss of autobiographical self occurs in Alzheimer's and other neurological disorders. General anesthesia also causes a temporary loss of autobiographical self.

Since we are primarily concerned with the effects of early-life abuse and trauma on the self, we must also look at the role of memory in the formation of the self. Schore (2003) asserts that memory is a psycho-physiological phenomenon. That is, it is not only cognitive but also somatic, a trauma that is stored in the body. Schore also maintained that *at the core of the self are affective processes.*

In the present model, these stored traumatic memories, or *engrams* (affective signatures in this context and usage), have energy that influences our sense of self throughout our lifetime. Unless directly confronted, these early trauma memories can continue to determine the course of one's life and sense of efficacy both individually and interpersonally. Shame is stored within this process.

Neurologically, then, the memory of early-life trauma and abuse, both pre- and post-verbal, are stored in the basal ganglia of the brain. Juxtaposed and slightly below the basal ganglia is the ascending reticular activating system (RAS) that not only regulates or maintains our consciousness but also sends neuronal impulse activity to the neocortex, allowing for our subjective sense of self (Damasio, 2010).

The relationship of the basal ganglia to the limbic system and especially the *amygdala* is evident in the sagital section of the brain as illustrated in Fig.2.1.

In the context of shame, children exposed to early-life abuse, trauma, and neglect appear to have highly reactive central nervous system (CNS) reactions to environmental cues perceived as threatening to them, typically called *fight-or-flight.*

In my clinical experience, these individuals as adults often present with histories of fractured relationships with parents, early-life sexual abuse or exploitation, and emotional isolation. The patients often say they believed they had to be "perfect" so that others wouldn't see their perceived flaws or "brokenness."

Their negative sense of self and their self-shame are frequently the basis of mood disorders such as depression.

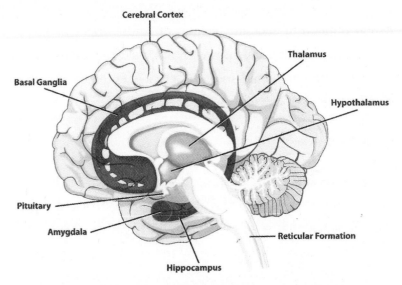

Figure 2.1. Illustration of relationship of basal ganglia to the limbic system. Illustration by Patti Laurrell, B.A.

Children who have suffered early-life trauma through neglect, violence, or physical and mental abuse may struggle to feel relieved, reassured, or safe throughout their lifetime; and they may engage in behaviors leading to addiction in their attempt to quell feelings of shame and inadequacy. Their damaged sense of self and toxic self-talk affirm their "brokenness."

Research suggests that a specialized affect-regulation system underpins feelings of reassurance, safety, and well-being (Gilbert, 2005). As we shall see in Chapter 5, Love vs. Abuse, healthy attachment appears to have a direct effect on our ability to register and respond to emotional cues with calmness and a sense of well-being and care—or with the opposite, a fear of attachment or loss. People with high levels of shame and self-criticism often have enormous difficulty being kind to themselves, feeling self-warmth, or being self-compassionate. They also find it very difficult to generate feelings of contentment, safety, and warmth in their relationships with others. Coincidental to deficits in one's ability to self-soothe is a lack of empathy or compassion for one's self and/or others.

Self-Talk

As the brain develops, so do *learned affective* reactions to the external environment and also to both positive and negative internal states that reinforce or inhibit negative affective reactions. The basis of self-talk is found in the internal states of early life. And as we develop into adults, we carry this internal voice with us. Negative self-talk and its attendant shame remain the same age (the age of trauma), and they never leave us.

Most writing about self-talk shares the common theme that our negative internal voice causes our painful emotional mood states. Cognitive-behavioral therapists believe that unpleasant feelings are a result of or a response to what our internal voice says to us. The voice that is typically judgmental and highly critical never tells us that we're okay or that we're doing a good job.

The thesis of this book is to wholly refute and empirically invalidate the clinical assumption that our internal dialogue, primarily negative self-talk, causes one's mood disorder or negative affective state. Rather, our negative self-talk is a function, expressed in words, of the early-childhood trauma.

The hypothesis proposed here is that primordial sensory receptors in the infant's brain, possibly at the level of the brain stem, record harmonic or disharmonic sensory-memory traces that prime an infant's response to stimuli—all at a preverbal level. Stimuli of a tactile or auditory nature are the primary suspects. Infants are also sensitive to the absence of tactile sensations. This all occurs prior to the development of descriptive language and symbol sets.

Language can provide only an approximation of human experience. It is through the developmental process that we learn to use verbal approximations to describe our sensory/affective state. When this state is tapped, as in psychotherapy, we see the age of the child's mental and emotional state—typically the age at which the early trauma, chaos, or crisis began. When we explore the content of self-talk, it is typically in response to early experiences that significantly formulated our own perception of self.

As we grow older and develop the ability to use language or symbol sets, we begin to define our primordial states through our identification with them. We learn the cultural labels of language and symbols to help us identify or define the early experiences that have affected us, especially traumatic events including sexual or physical abuse, chaos, abandonment, or violence toward our self or others.

The core primordial experiences build upon themselves as the brain develops, especially the prefrontal lobes and the limbic system. The role of the posteromedial cortices (PMC) is also critical in the development of consciousness (Damasio, 2010). This is how we become the grown-up, articulated version of our self, defined as the sum of our internal and external world experiences and our view of our own being that contains and perceives those experiences and our reactions to them.

Self-talk does not create our emotions or reactions to extreme criticism. Rather, self-talk is derived from the effects of early life and our developmental experiences in the world. When children are not praised, they do not develop in a healthy way. Children who are praised develop a sense of the "good me." Children raised in a critical, chaotic, or adverse environment develop a sense of the "bad me." Children raised in a hypercritical or violent environment develop a negative sense of self or self-worth and generalize that negativity socially by acting out. These children have a poor or nonexistent sense of trust, with themselves and especially with others. Alcoholism, drug addiction, and other negative forms of acting out often occur. Self-talk gives negative affirmation to these children's sense of self.

Negative self-talk does not, however, trigger or cause our moods, affective or cognitive disorders, or mental states. Negative self-talk just goes along for the ride! It is my core belief that most individuals suffering from depression, for example, do not know when or at what age their negative self-talk began. Foremost, I believe that the sense that something was not right emotionally was experienced first; negative self-talk began later.

Those exposed to early crisis typically do not remember the crisis but felt, or sensed, that something was wrong or painfully different. For example, did your mother confide in you as if you were her "little man" or "little woman"? Did she treat you as though you were older than you were? Did she treat you differently in these ways from how she treated your siblings? If she did, this role reversal was actually a form of child abuse. *Parentification* robs a child emotionally and psychologically by requiring the child to protect the parent and take sides. If you were parentified, can you recall how you felt about it? If you had negative feelings, they became a part of you before you could articulate them, but you inherently knew that something was wrong: "My parent should not be talking to me that way."

Anticipation and Distraction

Consciousness develops as a function of brain development; that is, the self develops as a function of differentiation through maturation. The self has the unique ability to think in the past, experience the present, and anticipate the future. Self-consciousness includes internal dialogue as well as thought and fantasy, which are different from self-initiated thinking. Self-talk is also one aspect of internal dialogue that can be hypercritical, especially toward the self.

Self-talk is frequently framed as anticipation, expectations, beliefs, and assumptions about people, situations and events now and in the future, and anticipated reactions to this expected future. People try to predict the future in an effort to be safe and secure in the knowledge of what's ahead. Some look forward with positive anticipation and excitement, while others who have experienced early-life trauma experience stress and anxiety, never feeling safe in what's ahead.

People whose self-talk is filled with reflections of the past are typically depressed in the present. They find no joy in their current lives and speak only of past events, often nostalgically. Individuals whose negative self-talk is about the future and "how things are going to be" are anxious about it, displaying anticipatory anxiety.

In contrast, people focused on the "now" and living in the present with little or no negative self-awareness or self-talk have a correspondent lack of negative affect. It is almost impossible to attach and hold on to a positive "in the now" experience if the brain is consciously and continuously negatively anticipating the next frame of our experience. Living in the now is transitory at best; we only stay there only in brief moments. In those moments, though, without negative self-talk, there is needed relief from the endless stimuli and distractions that hijack our attention and cause us to react with negativity during our entire waking state and throughout the night in our dreams.

Anyone who has either performed a monotonous task like folding laundry or had a "peak experience"—a moment of pure joy or ecstasy—knows what it's like to have the absence of negative thought. During that moment of "being, not thinking," we are at one with our self; at peace and in balance within our own universe, the pure self. As soon as we begin to recognize this monotony or bliss, however, we immediately lose the absence of negative thought. We begin to apply a value to our experience and are no longer in the moment. We have again engaged the beast!

How Do We Talk to Our Self?

One of the questions of interest in neuroscience considers which part of our consciousness or awareness allows or causes us to be able to talk to our self. To date, there is no definitive answer—only theories.

How do we separate our consciousness so that one part of it judges us but the other part is reactive to our self-judgments—and all of it is identified as the self? It seems incomprehensible that the judgmental voice and the reactive aspect are one and the same.

Negative self-talk is most often demeaning and full of fear. Fear is paralytic to our senses of self and security; it limits our range of responses to demands placed upon us. Our negative self-judgments keep us from reaching for the moon. As a sixty-five-year-old female patient, a former alcoholic with a chaotic early life, stated, "I think people are judging me, that I'm not okay; that I'm bad." This is what she was constantly telling herself, limiting her life's aspirations and attainments.

Treating Negative Self-Talk

Our reactions to self-judgments are preverbal and automatic: We fear without volitional control. We believe we are helpless, and *learned helplessness is a key feature of clinical depression* (Beck, 2009). Psychotherapy is about treating the primordial sense of self developed from our core sensory experiences, the early sense of inadequacy and helplessness for which language to describe or express this fails us as adults.

Our early emotional experiences as discussed within the psychotherapeutic process can only be expressed through an approximation of those original experiences. Therapists must allow patients to re-experience them psychoaffectively in treatment—not necessarily through age regression but quietly and by directing patients specifically to the original experience. Therapy is about being with patients as they explore their experience and their reactions to it, guiding them to look at the experience in myriad different ways and perspectives. Therapists help patients see that they now have the knowledge that they are okay and not alone, with the adult ability to handle these experiences in a way that affirms how they want to be and feel. This form of directed catharsis releases patients from the belief common to these patients that they are condemned and unable to change.

How Our Brain Creates Our Reality

For traumatized individuals, self-talk labels and blames the self as imperfect. The message is that perfection is necessary to avoid the shame that has colored the individual's perceptions and sense of self and self-worth.

Anxiety is a later feature of negative affective experiences. Unless it's free-floating, anxiety is associated with fear—either specific or generalized fear, as in generalized anxiety disorder. Anxiety involves the negative anticipation of an unpleasant event or affective experience.

Of deep interest in neuroscience is what is considered the "binding problem": how the brain integrates and maintains all of life's experiences as a whole. Freeman (1995, 1999), as discussed by Sander (2002), describes the brain as "constantly functioning to bring all experience, all training, all learning up to the present moment" [which Freeman calls the "now moment"] in antici-pating and organizing its next move. Thus, we have a brain that is constantly "putting it all together," constructing the present moment out of everything we have experienced in the past.

Mental life can be seen as a continuous process of expe-riencing, compiling, and storing information in the developing organism within its environment. Within the context of this interactive process of adaptation, Sander (2002) states that "although there are powerful moments of experiencing, they are couched within a context of previous moments and subsequent moments, which construct a flow of sequence and consequence that allows direction and meaning to be added to the experi-encing of the 'moment'" (26–27).

Neuroscience shows us that a primary function of the brain's recording of experience is to create our perception of our own reality. Through this process, conscious awareness takes place in the prefrontal, limbic, and posteromedial cortices, providing the circuitry that allows for the full panorama of our conscious experience (Damasio, 2010).

Regarding early experiences and the brain's developing morphology, Sander (2002) states,

> Of special significance is the interplay between an infant's experiencing and the developing morphology of the infant brain. For example, we are learning that the early experiencing of the infant shapes and

modifies the morphology of the baby's brain. Thus is opened the door to new understanding, both of long-term effects of certain negative features in an infant's early experiencing, such as trauma and recurrent pathogenic encounters, and on the positive side, amplifying the development of the brain's potential (16).

Thus, early-life experiences affect the brain's development and, in most respects, affect and determine one's unique sense of self as well as *how* we perceive. That is, the unique interaction of our brain's synaptic structures and our experiences as processed through the lens and filter of our brain affect not only our perception of the world but, more importantly, how we perceive our self. In support of this hypothesis, Damasio (2010) believes that feeling states are the simultaneous foundation of mind and self, namely the primordial feelings that describe the state of the organism's interior. "The front line of the explanation takes into consideration some critical facts. Feeling states first arise from the operation of a few brain-stem nuclei that are highly interconnected among themselves and that are the recipients of highly complex, integrated signals transmitted from the organism's interior.... In brief, in the complex interconnectivity of these brain-stem nuclei, one would find the beginning of an explanation for why feelings—in this case, primordial feelings—feel like something" (256–257).

How conscious of our self are we? For those struggling with toxic shame, self-knowledge and discovery are eclipsed by our own self-loathing or the defenses that attempt to mask it. We cannot put a Band-Aid on our affective wounds and make them go away; as we shall see in Chapter 6, "The Treatment of Shame," they must be discharged through confrontation with the abusers either directly or indirectly through guided imagery, hypnosis, and other affective discharging interventions.

The importance of self-awareness cannot be overemphasized. An orphan is someone with no ties to anyone living or dead. By becoming a psychological orphan, we are severing our psychological ties with anyone living or dead, thus gaining our own identity. As psychological orphans, we must be able to differentiate who we are from those early exposures or people who have affected us. This can help us gain a new perspective— an attempt to define our self in a way that allows us to grow emotionally rather than be stuck at the emotional age at which trauma and abuse began. As we shall see in Chapter 5, an experience doesn't have to be explosive to be traumatic or abusive. Trauma and abuse vary in degree and intensity.

An environment of abuse and trauma might be subtle and still have profound psychological, emotional, and social consequences.

CHAPTER 3

DEFINITIONS AND FOUNDATIONS OF AFFECTIVE LEARNING

Affects and the Basis of Shame: Infant Abuse, Trauma, and Neglect

Affect is the awareness of experiencing an emotional response to external stimuli. The stimulus may be as simple as a pinch or as complex as an eviction notice. As Picard et al. (2004) state in their comprehensive analysis of affective learning, "to date, there is no comprehensive, empirically validated theory of emotion that addresses learning.... Conducting controlled experiments dealing with affect has always been a challenge" (255).

It has been suggested that shame, or the mechanism for experiencing it, is born in us as a neural or biological affect. Gilbert and McGuire (1998) believe that shame is an innate capacity, while others believe that individuals are excessively prone to shame because of internal negative representations of self. These self-representations are derived from previous shaming experiences, manifesting themselves as a negative feed-back loop (Lewis, 1992; Nathanson, 1994).

In their exhaustive review of the literature regarding shame and early-life trauma, Matos and Pinto-Gouveia (2010) state, "Research has shown that shame-proneness seems to have trauma-like origins in negative rearing experiences, namely experiences of shaming, abandonment, rejection, emotional negligence, or emotional control, and several forms of abusive, critical, and/or harsh parental styles" (301).

According to Gilbert (2003), when a child experiences others' emotions directed at him, these shaming experiences become the foundation for self-beliefs and are recorded in autobiographical memory as emotionally textured experiences. These experiences can then become descriptors of the self, for example, "having elicited withdrawal in others and being treated as undesirable—therefore I am undesirable" (12–22).

Affects: The Foundation of Self

Let me be very clear: As presented in this model, *affects* are not emotions and should not be confused with emotions. Affects are the preconditions or neurological foundations for our ability to experience emotion. We cannot see, taste, touch, smell, or hear affects; we only experience them when they are activated. We hypothesize their existence through the display of emotion when the affect is triggered.

Most of us, whether we realize it or do not, are familiar with affects. We know about them primarily through how we feel and through the display of emotions—our own and those of others. An affect by definition is "the conscious subjective aspect of an emotion.... or a set of observable manifestations of a subjectively experienced emotion" (*Merriam-Webster online Dictionary*).

At a basic level, affects can be defined as the experience of feeling or emotion. Affect is a key part of the process of an infant's interaction with stimuli. The word affect has also been used to describe the display of emotions, which is "a facial, vocal, or gestural behavior that serves as an indicator of affect" (VandenBos, 2006, 26). Affect is also one of the three divisions of psychology: affective, behavioral, and cognitive.

For our purposes, however, affect will be defined as an *instinctual reaction to any stimulation occurring before the development of cognitive processes*. Affects are necessary for the establishment of the more complex emotions: fear, anger, sadness, happiness, disgust, and surprise.

In order to grasp the concept of affects and affective responses, simply stated, affects are *both* a place in the brain where certain early-life memory traces exist (e.g., trauma, abuse, neglect, abandonment) as well as a type of response when affects are triggered. There are two primary affective responses: shame and compassion. Compassion and its relationship to shame and psychotherapeutic interventions will be explored in depth in Chapter 6.

Affects are the substrate of our emotional makeup and are present at birth. They comprise the corpus of a child's preverbal experiences recorded in sensory memory even before birth.

Research shows that fetuses can learn as well as newborns. "Expectant moms who coo and chat to their babies while they're pregnant may be doing more than stimulating the fetus—they may be shaping their child's brain" (Holohan, 2013).

Affects are instinctual and preverbal reactions to stimuli. They are also intimately associated with arousal, which occurs in the basal ganglia of the brain stem and in the *amygdala*, part of the limbic system associated with emotional reactions and especially fight-or-flight reactions. Fight-or-flight reactions most often occur on an instinctual or primitive "survival" basis. Clinically, we see many individuals whose fight-or-flight reactions are directed toward protecting themselves emotionally. The amygdala regulates an instinctual reaction initiating this arousal process, either freezing the individual's response or accelerating mobilization if the individual experiences a threat.

Affects add significantly to the rich experience of living and sensing and to the unique quality of what makes us who and how we are. They are fundamental to the development and formation of the core self. A large part of what makes us human is our ability to feel and emote, to express our feelings. However, it's important to realize that feelings do not exist in a vacuum. There is always an object relationship involved: feelings are always feelings about or toward something.

Conversely, when affects are not present, individuals appear robotic, like zombies. Affects are absent during sleep, under general anesthesia, or in certain neurological conditions such as Alzheimer's disease, brain malformation, coma, or traumatic brain injury. In such cases, we can appreciate the importance of affect as it relates to the colorful expression and presentation of human life. We must, of course, be conscious, healthy, and aware as a precondition for affects to be fully experienced and expressed—and for life to be fully lived.

As we shall see in Chapter 5, children exposed to trauma, abuse, neglect, or abandonment have a heightened sense of threat or escape/avoidance behavior patterns even when no apparent threat is present. These same avoidant behavior patterns are also seen in individuals suffering from post-traumatic stress disorder (PTSD). Often, this hyperreactivity has no conscious underpinning or cognitive process when activated. It is like a knee-jerk reaction to a perceived threat to the individual's sense of self. Of particular interest is the fact that these traumatized children are also more prone to shame.

Learning Begins Early

All infants learn affectively prior to gaining knowledge through cognitive learning. Their first sensory experiences teach them about the world before they can put these experiences into words. Infants in healthy environments learn that crying can alert their caregivers to provide food, nurturing, and love. They grow secure by learning that there is a warm, responsive human being who will attend to their needs. Infants in unhealthy environments, however, learn the opposite. They cry without response and develop a helplessness and anxiety about the world around them. The root of all learning begins within the context of the bond between the parent/caregiver and the infant.

In her book on learning and the brain and her survey of the literature on infant learning, Smilkstein (2003) states, "A newborn recognizes the mother's voice, showing that the fetus, innately and naturally, without instruction or example, hears and remembers this particular voice" (52).

Further validation of the fact that infants learn early is supported by Branford, Brown, and Cockling (1999) in their two-year evaluation of research regarding the science of infant learning. They found that five- to twelve-week-old infants are "capable of perceiving, knowing, and remembering.... The answers about infant understanding of physical and biological causality, number, and language have been quite remarkable. These studies have profoundly altered scientific understanding of how and when humans begin to grasp the complexities of their worlds" (72).

Affective Learning Defined

All learning can be broadly defined as a change in behavior, the "modification of a behavioral tendency by experience (as exposure to conditioning)" (*Merriam-Webster online Dictionary*). All learning occurs on the following levels:

- Affective: related to self (sensory level of experience, preverbal)

- Experiential: knowledge-based (associative, conscious, cognitive)

Mosby's Medical Dictionary (2013) defines affective learning as "the acquisition of behaviors involved in expressing feelings in attitudes, appreciations, and values" (Mosby, 2013, 50). Based upon current research in neuroscience and developmental psychology, especially learning theory, it is my belief that affective learning is a nonconscious, preverbal, and precognitive response to any stimulus that affects the self-system—including genetic predispositions and congenital influences—of the child. The valence, or level of attractiveness, of such learning can be positive or negative in terms of the effects of the stimuli on the child. In other words, the child can exhibit both positive and negative behavioral responses to affectively charged stimuli.

The definition offered here is based on my belief that early-life primordial toxic experiences of the infant and child are neurologically encoded with the ability to affect the individual throughout life. This neurological encoding corresponds to an individual's response set in terms of the development of the primary self and the autobiographical self (Damasio, 2010).

In terms of the development of self, we can see that our temperament, bonding relationships with parents or caregivers, cognitive development, socialization patterns, and the idiosyncrasies of our family life and subculture interact in nonlinear terms. They are always influenced by our earliest experiences.

Affects and Learning

Researchers and educators have long known that there is more than one type of learning. Early attempts to identify types of learning were developed within the educational arena. In 1956, a committee of educational psychologists led by Benjamin

Bloom identified three easily understood domains or categories of educational activities: **Cognitive**—*knowledge,* **Affective**—*attitude,* and **Psychomotor**—*skills.* Bloom's Taxonomy of Learning Domains is still widely applied today. In the 1990s, a new group of cognitive psychologists led by Lorin Anderson, a former student of Bloom's, updated the taxonomy to reflect relevance to work taking place in the late 20th century (see Figure 3.1).

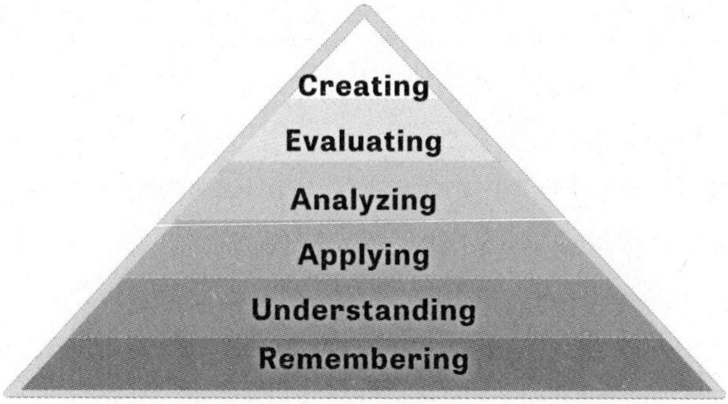

Creating

Evaluating

Analyzing

Applying

Understanding

Remembering

Figure 3.1. Updated Bloom's Taxonomy of Learning Domains
(Overbaugh and Schultz, n.d.)

Cognitive learning is the acquisition of knowledge and skills through mental and physical processes. We learn cognitively by listening, experiencing, watching, and doing, thereby gaining knowledge. We actively observe and interact with the world around us and learn from it. The cognitive domain involves knowledge and the development of intellectual skills. This includes the recall or recognition of specific facts, procedural patterns, and concepts that serve in the development of intellectual abilities and skills.

Through cognitive learning, we also learn the difference between right and wrong. We develop a moral code through the early bonding experiences with parents or caregivers. Guilt is the experience of knowing we have violated our moral code. We call this experience *transgression guilt*. Guilt, by definition, is a cognitive experience.

The affective domain, as defined by Krathwohl, Bloom, and Masia (1973), involves the manner in which we deal emotionally with things such as values, appreciation, enthusiasm, and other feelings, motivations, and attitudes. Affective learning precedes cognitive learning. The effects of affective learning are stronger than those of cognitive learning (knowledge-based learning). Affective learning is physiological and operates at a preverbal, nonconscious, sensory-motor level.

The psychomotor domain (Simpson, 1972) includes physical movement, coordination, and use of the motor-skills areas. Development of these skills requires practice and is measured in terms of speed, precision, distance, procedures, or techniques in execution (Clark, 2005).

Definitions of affective learning can be based only on the measures used to assess it. Without any empirical measurements for affective learning, we can only hypothesize its existence (Damasio, 2010). Current studies, however, are beginning to empirically demonstrate the nonconscious effects of affective learning on behavior. For example, Zemak-Ruger, Betman, and Fitzsimmons (2007) have demonstrated that emotional concepts can be primed without conscious awareness and remain inaccessible to conscious awareness yet still influence behavior in emotion-specific ways. Their findings also demonstrate that these effects persist over time.

With regard to the activation of nonconscious emotional concepts, these researchers have theorized,

> ... these concepts are represented by a network of nodes in the brain. Because of this network, the activation of a specific emotion makes related emotion-specific nodes more accessible and gives them a higher potential for affecting behavior. In other words, the activation of specific emotions causes the activation of emotion-specific linkages or concepts, which leads to an increase in emotion-specific behaviors (Zemak-Roger et al., 2007, 929).

Affect vs. Emotion

Emotions are complex events that are triggered by certain stimuli. A familiar smell or melody, such as peppermint or a holiday tune, can instantly make us feel nostalgic or sad or festive. Can we directly translate these complex emotions into words? We try, but we struggle to completely describe our emotions with our language. We can only approximate this subjective experience. Putting into exact words our overwhelming joy, bitter regret, or crippling anxiety—and all of the mental processes and effects of these emotions—can prove to be an impossible task.

To complicate things further, we may not know exactly how we feel or how many emotions are in play. It's both possible and normal to have several different emotions at the same time. These emotions may actually be competing with one another. As anyone who has sent a child off to college knows, it's possible to feel everything from happiness and pride to sadness and anxiety at the very same moment. Which, if any, of these emotions "wins"? How can we know or explain something like this?

Regarding the neurological differences between affect and emotion, Damasio (2010) states the following:

> A good rule of thumb suggests that we should reserve the term emotion for a reasonably complex program of actions (one that includes more than one or two reflex-like responses) triggered by an identifiable object or event, an emotionally competent stimulus. The so-called universal emotions (fear, anger, sadness, happiness, disgust, and surprise) are seen as meeting those criteria.

> The universality of emotional expressions reveals the degree to which the emotional-action program is unlearned and automated. The fact that emotions are unlearned, automated, and predictably stable action programs betrays their origin in natural selection and in the resulting genomic instructions (123).

Since they are responses to stimuli, emotions are an identifiable and, for the most part, organized affective states that seem to have a clear focus, the cause of which is usually known. Moods are also an affective state but are more diffuse, with no apparent focus. We can be in a certain mood—angry, sensitive, sad, depressed—for a prolonged period of time, but we often don't realize why.

Unlike emotions, moods can last for days, weeks, months, or even years! Depression, for example, is a mood disorder that can develop from the initial onset of symptoms into full-blown clinical depression if the symptoms last longer than two weeks. At this point, medication is often prescribed to treat the symptoms of depression, and talk therapy is a necessary component of this process.

We shall see in Chapter 6 what has been a theme throughout this book: The treatment of toxic shame requires identifying and dealing with the affective shame wounds associated with early-life abuse, trauma, and neglect.

CHAPTER 4
SELF-TALK

The Nemesis, and How It Begins

It's a fact of life that, surprisingly, many of us are unaware of: We all have a voice inside us that, for some of us, is a constant and often-critical companion. It has the capacity to exhaust our human energy and diminish our effectiveness as individuals. This voice is always with us and impossible to avoid. In a most bitter twist, our self-talk can in fact make us turn on our self! In troubled individuals, self-talk often turns into a highly malignant mind cancer that attacks its host, limiting the capacity to thrive. The ever-present voice could lead us down a ruthless, self-destructive path in which we become our own enemy. For its devastating effects alone and amplified by its constant presence, *the role of negative self-talk and its important influence on the human psyche cannot be overestimated.*

But where does all of this damaging force come from? The literature regarding negative self-talk and its origin, ironically, is rather sparse. Much of it is derived from anecdotal data or self-reported accounts from the addiction and twelve-step recovery world. Little empirical information is currently available regarding the nature of negative self-talk or its etiology. Not much is known about the phenomenological experience of this talk, especially how consciousness and self-awareness relate to our mental and emotional well-being. What is clear, however, is that within the context of addiction and recovery, *negative self-talk is about an individual's feelings of shame.* It's seen and understood as the result of exposure in early life to toxic and abusive environments.

Scientists are learning that trauma, abuse, neglect, abandonment, and other chronic violations to the self in early life develop and shape an individual's inner voice into an intrinsically negative instrument, darkening his or her world permanently. Sadly, physical, social, and emotional abuse frequently begin prior to an infant's verbal development, or before the first half of the second year of life. Think about the delicate state of the child at this point. In this particularly vulnerable stage, dependent children are still unable to fully communicate. They are at the mercy of the world around them. *When toxic exposures occur so early in life, in preverbal stages, they are stored as what I call "sensory signatures," or learned sensory reactions.* Each of us has a unique sensory signature based on our earliest experiences in life. As we shall see in Chapter 5, these experiences are stored as primordial imprints (signatures) in the brain stem during early development and are associated with a heightened startle response in infants. In other words, the experiences have a most significant impact on infants' developing brains, conditioning their reactions to everything, especially violations, or potential violations, to the self.

I prefer to use the term *sensory signature* to define preverbal or nonverbal affective imprints that are experienced and recorded as unique signatures and are associated with abusive or traumatic experiences from birth through early life. The signature is not random or undifferentiated. Rather, the stored signature is age-dated. *It is an affective profile that grows—but doesn't mature—and continues to be reexperienced throughout life, expressed in consciousness as the individual's internalized nemesis in its relationship to the self.*

It is my belief that self-talk derives its life both from and with a neurological substrate, that substrate being the basal ganglia of the brain combined with their rudimentary memory from early-life toxic exposures. The view of early-life trauma and abuse as the antecedents to the affective reaction of shame, with a defined neurological correlate, allows for a more empirical and clinical understanding of shame and leads to effective treatment approaches for shame and shame-based behavior. So much healing can begin with the critical realization that *negative self-talk is the voice of shame.*

We do not have to think about negative self-talk for it to exist—it seems to have a life of its own. The content of that life was born early in our development and experiences. The focus of this self-talk is directed specifically at and is only about one thing: the self. Its exact age is unknown. We can never remember when it began. How could we? It's always been with us as an affective imprint, stored from the abuses and neglect experienced when we were helpless and needing protection and love. It existed before we were aware of it.

When a child has been scorned, abused, or abandoned either physically, emotionally, or both—or even if a child feels unsupported in any way—the senses of self-worth and self-efficacy will both be low. When facing any kind of challenge as adults, these traumatized individuals react with rampant negative self-talk that leads to inevitable self-defeat. It's a sad and vicious cycle that keeps the individual from developing and succeeding in emotionally healthy ways. People can attempt an escape from this pattern of events, but typical escape behaviors (drinking, taking drugs, and other compulsive behaviors) usually only exacerbate their sense of shame. Their inner voice simply screams its disapproval of them. When they listen closely to the self-denigrating messages, they see self-loathing, disgust, and inadequacy coupled with feelings of mortification, exposure, and helplessness. The voice that has formed within them is very young, very scared, and very vulnerable indeed. *It doesn't reason or stop to reflect; it just is.*

In the available literature and anecdotal writing, negative self-talk is frequently portrayed as an internal voice disconnected from a person's early-life experiences, exposures, and trauma in particular. In fact, the etiology of self-talk is rarely discussed, especially as a biopsychosocial effect of early-life trauma and abuse. *The goal of this book is to provide an empirical foundation for the study of shame and its relationship to self-talk by demystifying the concepts surrounding it.* The present model of shame looks at it from the perspective of current neuroscience as having a biological foundation. To increase understanding, we will examine self-talk and shame from the standpoint of their psychosocial roots.

Self-Talk Is Irrational

To say that the content of negative self-talk is irrational is an understatement at best! At the heart of our critical inner voice is self-condemnation, the toxic self-identification that is associated with child abuse and trauma. These physical and emotional violations affect the basic emotional integrity of a child. In violent, hostile, or demeaning and abusive environments, children learn that they are not only unsafe but are also not "okay." The idea develops that something is intrinsically wrong with them. The basic language of negative self-talk supports this connection at every turn. Self-talk turns us against our self and our own best interests, which in itself is irrational. To understand the etiology of self-talk, we make the assumption that infants start out *tabula rasa*, a blank slate. We also know that the irrational imprints of our inner critic are a function of early trauma of one type or another. Universally, children do not volitionally build an irrational and debilitating inner voice. Why would they? Their natural instinct is to survive and grow, to be free of chronic and uncompromising conflict. They violate that instinct only with the help of an abusive, unsupportive, violent, or chaotic early-life environment. Healthy environments provide a stable foundation upon which children can grow and develop into healthy adulthood. Children exposed to trauma and abuse grow on a threatening and self-defeating foundation. These children develop into adults who never feel safe or protected. They are emotionally vulnerable at every turn.

Theoretical Origins of Self-Talk

The uncharted universe of the infant's mind and experiential processes continues to be a source of interest to behavioral scientists, child-development professionals, and educators. Since infants lack symbolic understanding, language, and a sense of self, they are unable to communicate their internal state in their interactions with the world around them. We can only infer or hypothesize causal relationships in an infant's world, since babies cannot tell us how they feel or what they are experiencing. Despite this fact, *neuroscience is beginning to show us that affects are part of our nervous system at birth* (Damasio, 1999, 2010). To help us understand how and what environmental factors impact us in terms of memory, learning, and experience, we can rely only on observation, inference, and anecdotal data. These factors aid in our understanding of environmental impacts in early development.

The model presented here asserts that the neurological substrate of self-talk resides in the basal ganglia of the brain stem. Basal ganglia are directly associated with the activation of the central nervous system. In infancy and early childhood, preverbal affects—emotional/sensory signatures—are stored in the basal ganglia as what we might call memory traces. Mosby (2013) defines *affect memory* as "a particular emotionally expressed feeling that recurs whenever a significant experience is recalled" (50), but these memory traces are undifferentiated in babies primarily because infants are unable to consciously identify emotions. Babies also lack language for conscious negative self-talk at this age.

As the infant develops, the affective signature of abuse in particular also develops through language and becomes what we call shame. Self-talk develops from preverbal affects in the basal ganglia of the brain stem that are associated with activation. Children who have been abused, neglected, abandoned, or in any way subjected to cruelty or trauma appear to be highly sensitized and frequently experience heightened startle reactions and emotional activation. In the past, we referred to these children as being "high-strung or nervous."

All of these factors create in the abused child a heightened sense of alarm or activation. Children who have suffered abuse and violation of any kind also typically experience low self-esteem. As adults, these same individuals present in therapy with damaged psychological and emotional integrity and symptoms including depression, anxiety, panic, and shame (often experienced as shame attacks). Shame-based behavior is a common feature in the clinical picture of abused infants and children.

As previously stated, the harmful affective processes of negative self-talk are preverbal. They can possibly occur even before birth. Studies have shown that an unborn child can hear sounds as early as twenty weeks, turning toward the sounds of its parents' voices. It will be startled, perhaps even traumatized, by loud noises at about twenty-five weeks (Holohan, 2013). Very loud sounds can even cause changes in a baby's heart rate and movements.

Early abuse and trauma are directly associated with shame. When children are violated in any way, their forming sense of self and self-safety are damaged developmentally. Erikson's model of psychosocial development (1950) clearly established the ontological developmental patterns from birth through old age. In his model, shame develops between the ages of two and three, while guilt, being a later feature of development and directly related to language, shows itself between the ages of three and five. Thus, shame is a part of our psyche, of who we are. Toxic shame is associated with early-life trauma, abuse, neglect, and abandonment—either physical, emotional, or both.

The internal chatter of negative self-talk frequently communicates a sense of inadequacy and a deep fear of abandonment in affected individuals. Never being "good enough" is a feature paramount in these individuals. The thought process is "If I'm myself, people won't accept me or like me." *Self-doubt is a constant reminder of our vulnerability and sense of somehow being defective—not good enough, flawed.* The language of negative self-talk is made up of all the words formed by negative affects very early in life. They are illogical and irrational. What child would intentionally experience self-loathing, let alone promulgate that throughout his or her life?

Critical Self-Talk and Guilt Are Not the Same

Guilt and shame are often perceived to be associated with

each other. However, the literature, as we shall explore later, supports the differentiation of shame and guilt as separate experiences that are not coterminous. Self-talk has its roots in and is directly associated with shame and cyclical shame-based behavior. Guilt, on the other hand, is associated with conscience and conscious thought. *Guilt is about an infraction of our values, while shame is about our self.*

As asserted in the model presented in this book, the etiology of critical self-talk is the result of early-life abuse and trauma. Negative self-talk expresses shame toward the *self*. To the contrary, guilt is often experienced as anxiety about infracting a learned value; it is not about the self at all. Guilt is about something we did; shame is always about us, about who and how we are.

In positing that there is a definite distinction between critical self-talk and a conscience (guilt), Firestone et al. (2002) state the following:

> It is important to remember that the [critical] voice is not a conscience or a moral guide. The voice is irrational, illogical, and contradictory: First, it influences us to act in self-defeating ways, and then it condemns us for those very actions. In effect, the voice puts us in a no-win situation. In addition, if the voice were a true conscience, it would not have a tone of sarcasm or ridicule nor would it possess a harsh, punishing quality. The "shoulds" and the "ought tos" that we experience from the voice exert a heavy pressure on us, undermining our energy and motivation rather than inspiring us to try to change actions we recognize as being self-defeating or self-destructive (42).

The Age of Self-Talk

There can be no self-talk without the development of language skills. In the majority of infants, language develops in the first half of the second year of life. In the preverbal stage of development, before children understand the words or symbol sets of their culture, they have sensory experiences. The sensations infants feel are internal, and they are also shaped by external stimuli from their undifferentiated environment. The infant is essentially a preverbal, stimulus-bound reactor!

As the brain develops, so do learned affective reactions to the external environment—and to positive and negative internal states that reinforce or inhibit negatively affective reactions. *The basis of self-talk is found in the internal states of early life.* If infants feel comfortable, they are calm and quiet. If infants are uncomfortable, they can be soothed by a parent's or caregiver's attention to their needs. These early feelings of comfort or distress feed the development of a child's reactions and feelings of safety and well-being. These feelings are the preverbal precursors to an individual's self-talk.

Self-talk is possible only with the development of language or symbol sets used to communicate with our inner selves. Language is inadequate, however, to describe painful sensory experiences in our early lives. Words only derive meaning through conventional use and standards, but these early experiences affect and shape us before we have this ability to verbally express our self.

When we listen to our negative self-talk, are we really

listening to our self at our current age? Or are we hearing and experiencing feelings and sensations from an earlier age? Is it the age at which our emotional development was short-circuited? Or is it the age when we began to feel there was something wrong or different about us? It could quite possibly be the age when trauma or loss occurred in our lives. If the crisis and chaos lasted a long time, *the developmental voice will be of that age*—the time or age the trauma was initially experienced. Most patients discussing early-life events do not typically recall the exact age they were, unless there was a specific experience or milestone at the time. Usually, however, the traumatic experiences or abusive events lasted long enough to leave an indelible mark on the individual's sense of self and security.

Pia Mellody's groundbreaking work regarding the relationship of early-life trauma and codependent behavior alludes to the stored memory of primordial sensory experience:

> As a result of experiencing abuse in childhood, we spend a lot of energy in adult life trying to avoid encountering the intolerable reality from the past. But the unpleasant reality is within us anyway. At one level, we know and feel something about it and we've known and felt something about it before— even if we can't consciously face and describe it. And the presence of this repressed reality makes us tend to avoid unpleasant feelings in the present. Our physical bodies look adult, but our inner feelings and thinking are immature, fearful, and confused. The difference between our external reality and internal reality generates stress and pain that are difficult to deal with. Codependents often drift into an addiction,

physical illness, or mental illness to medicate or remove these painful feelings" (1989, 55).

Therapy is about helping patients understand the emotional age or affective level at which they are listening to themselves.

The perfectionism and shame-based self-talk of one of my patients, a thirty-eight-year-old female physician, resembled that of a withdrawn and frightened three-year-old—the age at which her maternal uncle had her perform fellatio on him. As time passed, she couldn't tell anybody out of fear: fear of ridicule and the fear of disgrace and abandonment. As she developed into an adult, a sense of inadequacy also developed and grew. Regardless of her academic and professional accomplishments, she heard only her traumatized three-year-old self. Her fate was sealed by shame. Even repeating the word *shame* during therapy initially caused withdrawal reactions in her. After two hospitalizations for major depressive disorder, she entered therapy. She objectified anything that might have been construed as emotion in a detached, clinical way. As she progressed, she was able to understand the relationship between her early-life sexual trauma and her emotionally-avoidant personality style.

Self-Talk Is Not the Same as Thinking

Thought and self-talk are not the same. Thought is volitional and involves a particular choice or purpose. We have to *think* about thinking. Thought is also associated with consciousness. Critical self-talk is passive and negatively oriented, influencing our perception of our self and others. We don't hear any positive or affirming statements from our critical self-talk. It reflects value judgments and critical self-evaluation. These are most likely the negative judgments developed through early shaping processes by parents, caregivers, or peers and the environment in which they occurred.

The negative judgments and critical self-talk are about our adequacy, self-worth, or emotional states. Undeniably, self-talk is born out of our emotional experiences, and its etiology is the sum of our early exposures. Our self-talk is caused by, and subsequently also drives, our emotional states. *Once we are able to label something in our self, we react to that self-characterization as an object, often with ridicule and scorn.*

Regarding our self-judgments and self-talk, Don Miguel Ruiz and Don Jose Ruiz so clearly asserted in *The Fifth Agreement*:

> Your tyrant is ruthless. It's always abusing you by using all those symbols against you. It thrives on emotional poison generated by negative emotions, and the way it generates these emotions in you is by judging and giving opinions. Nobody judges you more than you judge yourself. Of course, you try to escape from the judgment, the guilt, the rejection, and the punishment. That's why so many people overeat, take drugs, abuse alcohol, and become addicted to various substances and behaviors (2010, 108).

We Begin to Understand

We have learned that the voice inside us can often be negative, critical, and self-defeating. Because of its dramatic debilitating effects, it's important to understand this self-talk, its sources, and its reason for existence. Cognitive scientists are learning more about brain development and the effects of abuse or trauma in infants. A clearer picture is emerging regarding the effects of early-life abuse, subjective emotional affects, negative sensory reactions, and self-worth.

We see that infants developing in toxic environments—before they can even talk—will develop stronger startle responses and higher sensitivity to their environment. They will react with sensory signatures: negative imprints on their brain and psyche. It is here that the dangerous cycle of negative self-talk and its language of shame begins. Children who experience emotional damage start to perceive themselves as inherently defective, broken, and unworthy of love and affection from others. The painful cycle of our inner negative dialogue, *the talk of shame*, is born.

It's not about guilt, or feeling bad about something we've *done*, that goes against our values. It's about our most primal perception of our self and, therefore, is much more significant. We now understand that most people, including the most traumatized individuals, have no idea of the developmental age of their inner verbal demon or even its existence at first. Their affective profile was constructed before they were old enough to realize it. It is a part of them in every way.

The importance of exploring, seeking, and finding the source of negative self-talk through therapy is critical. A patient has to identify the development of that voice in order to begin understanding, questioning, and eventually—with much effort and guided therapy—starting to defeat it. Shame is intrinsic, making it a formidable opponent, to say the least. But toxic shame can be challenged, worked through, and eventually defeated. The possibility of victory against toxic shame inspired this book; and we've completed the first step to overcoming it: recognizing and beginning to understand it and its sources.

Josh's Story

Robert and Jamie met at a school orientation when they were both sixteen. The two young people attended a well-known school for the handicapped. Both Robert and Jamie suffered from *retrolental fibroplasia* (RLF), which is blindness as the result of hyperoxygenation of their incubators at birth. Their school friendship soon developed into a romantic relationship.

At seventeen, Jamie became pregnant; and just before her eighteenth birthday, she gave birth to Josh. Robert's father, Philip, was adamant that neither Robert nor Jamie had the psychological or emotional maturity to provide a healthy and stable environment within which to raise Josh. Furthermore, their adolescent relationship became fraught with acrimony once Jamie became pregnant and decided to keep the baby. Robert was afraid this would ruin his college plans and future career goals; he wanted to teach the visually disabled.

Robert's mother and father were partners in their own business-consulting firm and spent considerable time working outside the country. Nonetheless, they were not going to abandon their grandson. With the consent of Jamie and her parents, they adopted Josh at birth and raised him as their own. Josh called his grandparents Mom and Dad.

Josh presented for treatment at twenty-seven years old, in significant emotional pain. A college graduate with a degree in graphic design and a well-paying job as a designer with a well-known firm, he had completed three years of counseling with a local psychotherapist. He felt that he needed more than cognitive-behavioral therapy for what he reported as "severe shame." He felt that he and his therapist had gone about as far as they could go together.

Josh reported that when he was six months old, his "parents" adopted a male child, Jesse, from Honduras and raised the infant as his brother. When Josh was four years old, his mother and father became foster parents to an eight-year-old female child, Stacey, whose mother was a drug addict and a distant cousin of the family.

Between the ages of two and fifteen, Josh stated that he was actually raised by his Honduran nanny, Reina, as his parents were out of the country a lot to see clients. Reina passed away two years before Josh presented for therapy, having moved back to Honduras after being diagnosed with brain cancer. Josh stated that he's been unable to grieve for her even though she had played a central role in raising him and provided love when everything else around him was unsafe and fearful.

Josh said that between the ages of six and thirteen, he'd been verbally and sexually abused by his adoptive sister, Stacey. "What began as her coming into my room and simply fondling me at night turned into sexual abuse every day," he said. "Every fucking day, I came home to be sexually abused by her.”

When Josh was thirteen, he told his parents as well as Reina about the ongoing sexual abuse. Reina was powerless to help him; and his father was completely passive, avoidant, and totally codependent on his wife. His mother’s response was, “She wasn’t really family anyway.” Josh was given no emotional support or empathy for what he had experienced in his own home. He felt that the people he’d always considered his parents minimized the seriousness of his sexual abuse.

“My mother called me stupid—I was treated as a low-grade person in the house,” he said. “My stepbrother got all the favors of my parents.”

Josh saw very little of his biological parents between the ages of five and thirteen. They were no longer together and were living out of state. During the summers, his adoptive mother took Josh see his biological father. His biological mother did not want to see him or be a part of his life, so Josh never saw her after the age of six. Josh’s biological father remarried when Josh was thirteen, and Josh couldn’t integrate into the new family. After the age of thirteen, he never saw his father again. The emotional abandonment and abuse have left him with crippling emotional scars.

At sixteen, Stacey was admitted into a rehabilitation facility for chemical dependency and subsequently disappeared. Josh was, therefore, never able to confront her.

Josh said that his negative self-talk began when he was five or six and continued through high school with thoughts of his being a “fraud” or a “phony.” Josh was aware now of how toxic that self-talk had been but described it then as becoming "normal thought." He was determined not to act on it, but it was a battle.

"I struggle not to surrender to others—I hardly feel strong about anything," he said. "I find ways to cut myself down—I never get myself to believe what I think. It's driving me crazy." Josh felt like his world could be taken away from him at any time.

The sexual violation he'd suffered by his sister, the brutalization and bullying by his brother throughout middle school, and more bullying by his middle school classmates, combined with the lack of support from his parents, made Josh what he called "a very suicidal kid."

"I once tried to drown myself and another time walked in front of a car," he said. Josh reported that his brother is now an alcoholic and lives in a nearby town. They have no contact whatsoever with each other.

Josh retained only fragments of his childhood and couldn't remember or describe how he felt about the abuse." I have blank years," he said. "Between six and twelve, I have practically no memories."

At the start of his therapy, Josh's issues around trust were manifest. "I don't trust anybody. I don't think I know what trust is," he said. "My mother made me feel like I was incapable of doing the simplest things. She was relentless. I don't know what it means to be myself and trust myself—I don't know what it looks like or feels like. Internally, I don't feel like I have a right to be assertive. Everything about me is surface."

Josh also described a disconnect with the here and now. "I

find I'm in my head a lot," he said. "It's all anticipatory thinking—I'm rarely in the now. Maybe it's because I'm angry and I
feel robbed."

Josh's compassion-based therapy focused on issues of
trust as well as his anger and rage regarding the sexual abuse
and the lack of support from his family. Since his parents were
now advanced in age and both were in poor health and financial
distress, Josh became able to communicate with them and deal
with their needs on a healthy, more adult level without compro-
mising his own needs.

However, Josh still found it difficult to feel intimate as well
as confident. "I feel shame after intimacy," he said. "My sexuality
is weird. I have incestuous thoughts, I have bisexual thoughts,
and I don't think I know what sex is; but I do know that I'm very
intimidated by women that I see as powerful."

Despite this feeling, Josh had met a female student at
college; and they dated for six years, with the intention of
marrying. However, Josh stated that it was still difficult for him
to relax sexually without feeling judged.

As therapy progressed, Josh reported having more "regular
self-talk" and what seemed to him to be "a kinder self-talk." "I
don't think in words—I think in images," he said. "I'm trying
to escape my destiny of failure. I'm trying to change habits, my
relationships, and be more true to myself."

To that end, Josh made exceptional progress. He married
his longtime girlfriend and began raising his own family.

CHAPTER 5
LOVE VS. ABUSE

Authentic Love Begins with Self-Love

Love is critical for a person's healthy physical, emotional, social, and psychological development. It affects all of who anyone is. The importance of love in early-life development cannot be overstated, especially love's relationship to shame and its accompanying wounds.

Even with the prosaic aspects and definitions of love, which are probably all correct, love is an affectional response from or for another—a feeling. The antecedents of what people term *love* must reside within them before they can convey or project love to someone else. In essence, that which someone calls love is actually a projection of how that person feels about the self—but directed toward another.

The affectional response of love in all of its aspects and elements must be experienced internally in order for people to be able to project outward what they feel toward their self. If they do not have healthy self-love, then by default, they cannot project or convey authentic love toward another.

People most often associate the idea of self-love with narcissism, arrogance, self-centeredness, and hubris. As used here however, self-love is associated with healthy self-associations and positive self-talk. Ideally, self-love and self-care mean freedom from internal conflict, which is usually and fundamentally about the same thing: who and how a person is.

Conversely, individuals whose earliest life experiences are associated with abuse, neglect, violence, abandonment, or trauma most often experience what we have called "affective wounds," which upset the development of healthy self-love. For these unfortunate individuals, this affects everything that follows, especially romantic attachments.

The Foundations

In his presidential address to the American Psychological Association (1958), Harry Harlow's speech was titled "The Nature of Love." His presentation was a synthesis of his groundbreaking research regarding maternal attachment and nurturing.

A series of Harlow's experiments forever changed our understanding of the role that touch and affection play in the healthy development of both primate and human infants. Harlow demonstrated the powerful human need for love. By showing the devastating effects of maternal deprivation on young rhesus monkeys, Harlow's research demonstrated the importance of a mother's love for healthy human childhood development and especially self-love.

The Studies

Harlow's primary group of experiments involved the exposure of rhesus monkeys separated from their mothers at birth and caged alone in the lab. They were allowed no physical contact with lab personnel, yet they were able to see other monkeys and lab staff. These isolated monkeys quickly began to exhibit abnormal symptoms such as clutching themselves, staring into space, rocking repeatedly, and injuring themselves by biting themselves or their cages. These monkeys did not groom themselves or play, and they were prone to depression. The baby monkeys were then assigned to one of two different mother surrogates. One was made of chicken wire with a soft terrycloth covering, a round head, two eyes, monkeylike ears, and a mouth but did not provide any food. The other "mother" was made of chicken wire with a frightening crocodilian head and milk provided from an attached baby bottle.

The results showed that baby monkeys spent significantly more time with their cloth mother than with the wire mother that dispensed milk. Harlow concluded that "'contact comfort' is a variable of overwhelming importance in the development of affectional response, whereas lactation is a variable of negligible importance" (1958, 676). These babies needed warmth and comfort significantly more than nourishment.

Harlow further demonstrated in another series of experiments that their affectional responses to these mother-surrogate terrycloth comfort monkeys also allowed the baby monkeys to learn and experience healthy separation and affiliative behaviors as adults.

Regarding the longitudinal effects of healthy bonding, Harlow concluded that "human affection does not extinguish when the mother ceases to have intimate association with the drives in question. Instead, the affectional ties to the mother show a lifelong, unrelenting persistence, and even more surprising, widely expanding generality" (673–674). Thus, maternal bonding is essential for healthy growth and development; furthermore, the effects of healthy bonding also persist into adulthood and lead to mature socialization and mating.

As a basic affectional or love variable, contact comfort is essential and even more important than milk. In that regard, one primary function of the "real" mother, and presumably of a mother surrogate whether subhuman or human, is also to "provide a haven of safety for the infant in times of fear and danger. The frightened little child clings to its mother, not its father, and this selective responsiveness in times of distress, disturbance, or danger may be used as a measure of the strength of affectional bonds" (678).

Psychosocial development is also highly dependent upon the child's sense of safety and adequacy. Through healthy bonding and attachment, children begin to develop their sense of autonomy, individuation, and independence, secure in their interactions with the outside world.

As we shall see in the next section, psychosocial development is more complex than its objective behavioral manifestations. Bonding and emotional growth are equally dependent upon our brain's neurochemical contribution.

Oxytocin: The Neurochemical Binder of Bonding

Harry Harlow could not have anticipated that the neurological basis of all mammalian bonding was a hormone and neuropeptide secreted directly into the blood from the posterior lobe of the pituitary gland (Forsling, 2001).

As we shall see, oxytocin is the primary and essential component and factor within the bonding process. The hormone was discovered in 1909 by the English physiologist Sir Henry H. Dale. He found that an extract from the human posterior pituitary gland caused uterine contractions in a pregnant cat. Oxytocin is found "unchanged in every mammalian species" (Dalton, 2005).

A half century after its discovery, the biochemist Vincent du Vigneaud synthesized oxytocin; it is now frequently prescribed under the brand names of Pitocin and Syntocinon to augment or induce labor (Dalton, 2005).

In her book *The Oxytocin Factor* (2003), Kerstin U. Moberg, M.D., Ph.D., suggests that oxytocin is the primary hormone that calms the body and promotes social bonding. Moberg asserts that oxytocin has the opposite effect of the "fight-or-flight" hormones vasopressin and adrenaline, which trigger stress, danger readiness, and weariness or distrust of strangers. Moberg further asserts that oxytocin facilitates relaxation and encourages romantic, family, and pair bonding.

The importance of oxytocin in the bonding process cannot be overestimated. From the standpoint of an individual's emotional development and from what we already know, oxytocin appears to be a primary factor associated with an individual's ability to feel safe emotionally as well as in social relationships. In fact, we know the importance of eye contact in interpersonal relationships, and it's often revealed in the clinical setting as well. Patients who feel safe can share a gaze and not deflect eye contact. Similarly, as a mother looks at her child and the child reciprocates, that visual connection forges within mother and child a nonverbal neural connection that evokes a feeling of safety in the infant. At that moment, oxytocin is released within both mother and infant. As the infant grows and develops, corresponding neuronal connections associated with the release of oxytocin increase along with the memory of the association with mother or surrogate.

As a result of oxytocin's effect during the bonding process, children are able to experience the positive affective bond associated with their mother even in her absence. In their work with adult attachment issues, Levine and Heller (2010) point out the significant interest in oxytocin in recent years, especially in the press, via the part it plays in attachment processes. Oxytocin, say the authors, "serves several purposes: It causes women to go into labor, strengthens attachment, and serves as a social cohesion hormone by increasing trust and cooperation. We get a boost of oxytocin in our brain during orgasm and even when we cuddle— which is why it's been tagged the 'cuddle hormone'" (251-252).

Conversely, if the bonding process is either absent or broken in infancy or childhood from abandonment, trauma, neglect, or violence, these individuals as adults frequently experience significant interpersonal conflict, avoidance, and distrust, both of self and others. Violence toward self or others may also be a part of their acting-out behavior. Bullying is not uncommon among these individuals, either as victims, perpetrators, or both. They often experience low self-worth and self-esteem, frequently feeling "less than" and unloved. In the extreme, clinicians often see the clinical effects of reactive attachment disorder as well as many addictive disorders.

Ironically, as Levine and Heller (2010) point out, "by forgoing closeness with our partners, we are also missing our oxytocin boost—making us less agreeable to the world around us and more vulnerable to conflict." (252).

As psychotherapists, we see the devastating effects of broken bonds, lost attachments, and trauma in patients who present with addictions, compulsive disorders, anxiety, depression, and other mood and clinical disorders. Patients' histories frequently reveal voids or ruptures in their relationships with their mother or surrogate mother, presupposing that a mother figure was even present.

Individuals' stories frequently present with themes of feeling emotionally unsafe or insecure, parenting themselves or being overly parentified or losing a sense of childhood by meeting the parent's needs instead of their own needs as a child. Any of these situations can cause them to feel that their needs are unimportant, leading to a loss of self. In discussing this void, spiritual psychologist John Welwood (2000) states, "The core wound we all suffer is the disconnection from our own being" (16).

Because of this disconnection, individuals feel damaged,

unsafe, and inadequate to meet life's challenges. Frequently denying and/or overcompensating for their vulnerability and isolation, these people often resort to alcohol or drugs to quiet their demeaning, shame-inducing internal chatter. The inner voice often reveals the voice of their abuser; this is a voice that is definitely not an element of love but rather an enemy of their self.

Bradley's Story

Bradley, a thirty-two-year-old Caucasian male, had come to treatment on his own. He was a high school graduate who hadn't attended college but was moderately successful as a sales and product manager. Bradley stated that he had sought therapy around twelve years ago but admitted that he attended only one session. This time, his motivation for treatment centered around three primary issues: anger, depression, and insomnia. He added that he lacked confidence.

When asked about his interpersonal relationships, Bradley indicated that he had several male friends but he started dating only two months before his first therapy appointment and that his girlfriend, whom he met in a bar, is four years his senior. He said that he was just a social drinker but admitted to smoking marijuana daily. "I'm addicted to pot—it numbs my feelings," he said. "After twelve years of heavy drug use, I don't know who I am."

When Bradley was two years old, his father committed suicide on his fortieth birthday. He became drunk and shot himself in front of Bradley's mother and two half-sisters. Bradley's paternal grandfather had also committed suicide with a gun.

When asked about further traumatic childhood memories, Bradley said that when he was seven years old, his mother and stepfather broke up and then got back together again.

"I was worried that my mother and stepfather would divorce and I would be abandoned," he said. It was obvious that his biological father's violent and tragic ending weighed heavily in his thoughts throughout his life.

Bradley recalled wanting to commit suicide as a sophomore in high school.

"I felt very alone—I wanted to kill myself, but I didn't because my dad killed himself and that would hurt my mom," he said. "I needed to protect my mother even though I was never protected."

When asked to elaborate on his statement of feeling unprotected, Bradley revealed with anger that his mother had used him as an emotional buffer between her and his stepfather. He said that she had offered him no protection and that he had felt frightened much of the time. They had moved often, and he had never felt safe in one place. He stated that anger is a major problem for him. "I sabotage relationships long-term," he said. "I'm very self-deprecating, and I have a lot of shame. I hate myself, but I want to be the best and master myself."

Bradley's fear of intimacy was seen as directly related to his parentification by both mother and stepfather. This, coupled with his sense of isolation and aloneness, resulted in his inability to develop healthy relationships as well as have a clear perception of himself. Pushing people away was the only way Bradley knew how to cope. It appeared that his emotional development ceased to grow; and as an adult, he became dependent upon drugs to alleviate his mood and anger issues.

Unconditional Love

Writing on the conditionality of love, Welwood (2000) states the following:

> The parent-child relationship provides our first experience of the confusing ways in which conditional and unconditional love become mixed up. Although most parents originally feel a vast, choiceless love for their newborn child, they eventually place overt or covert conditions on their love. This is used as a way of controlling the child, turning their [parental] love into a reward for [the child's] desired behaviors. The result is that as children, we rarely grow up feeling loved for our self just as we are. We internalize the conditions our parents put on their love, and the internalized parent (the superego, or "inner critic") often rules our lives. We keep trying to placate this inner voice, which constantly judges us as never good enough (254).

Clearly, self-love cannot grow and develop when the environment is not facilitative. The preconditions for love are a sense of comfort and safety. Trauma and abuse, on the other hand, create the opposite of safety and security for an infant or a child; for example, infants who have been abandoned are affected at a preverbal level. Infants do not have language for a psychological schema within which to frame loss. The loss is then experienced physiologically through the senses. In addition to the psychological effects of early life, the effects in adulthood can be reexperienced in stressful times through somatic complaints such as headaches, stomachaches, chest or lower body pain, and stress pains, especially around the neck area.

Childhood Trauma and Abuse

In the present model, trauma is any event, contact, or experience in which the child's internal and external resources are inadequate to cope with the external threats to the self. According to Janise DiCiacco (2007), a pioneer in the area of childhood-attachment disorder, uncontrollable disruptions or distortions of attachment precede the development of posttraumatic stress syndrome. DiCiacco emphasizes that there are four common behavioral and emotional responses that parents and teachers frequently witness in children who have experienced trauma:

- Difficulties in modulating or tempering strong emotions related to the trauma, such as anger, grief, and irritability

- Difficulties in maintaining connections with others

- Difficulties with the ability to soothe or comfort one's self

- Difficulties with the ability to maintain a positive self-identity

Childhood abuse and neglect enhance long-term hyperarousal and decrease modulation of strong affect (DiCiacco,

2007, 47). Thus, children exposed to trauma and neglect have nervous systems requiring higher external stimulation in order for the brain to produce calming endogenous opioids in times of crisis and stress as opposed to the comfort provided by the responses based on good or healthy caregiver experiences.

Complex trauma as described by Beckert-Weidman, Ehrmann, and LeBow (2012), also called *developmental trauma disorder*, typically involves multiple traumatic experiences such as ongoing physical, emotional, or sexual abuse; abandonment by the caregiver; chronic or severe neglect; domestic violence; and witnessing death or gruesome injuries as a result of community violence, terrorism, or war. Beckert-Weidman et al. further emphasize that complex trauma's defining factor is that it involves chronic early-childhood maltreatment (e.g., physical abuse, neglect, or failure of protection) within a caregiving relationship. The maltreatment's effects are so damaging and pervasive because they are delivered by the caregiver. Because these events are chronic and occur early in life, they further erode and damage a child's normal developmental processes. Beckert-Weidman et al. have identified seven domains of impairments resulting from early-life trauma:

- Attachment
- Biology
- Emotional regulation
- Behavioral regulation
- Defenses
- Cognition
- Self-concept (71)

It is clear from the above that children fail to thrive emotionally when continuously exposed to conflict and chaos, especially when issues associated with attachment are present. As we have seen in our earlier discussion of Harlow's studies, attachment disorders on the human level develop in the first two years of life. By age two, children develop a mental representation of their caregivers (DiCiacco, 2007).

What happens when the caregiver is emotionally or physically absent—or worse: violent, abusive, and unable to bond with the child? Welwood (2000) asserts that ego defenses are built in the spaces where love is absent. These defenses attempt to protect individuals from emotional pain but instead contribute to their separation from their self by blinding them to the realities of their own feelings and critically skew their perceptions of their self. Ironically, humans so often live in a darkness created by their own need to feel safe and secure.

With regard to disorders of attachment or bonding, these defenses typically display a commonality of behaviors and reaction styles. Children with reactive attachment disorder typically present with the following behaviors (Beckert-Weidman et al., 2012, 71):

- Inability to form meaningful attachments and relationships

- Inability to trust self and others

- Failure to develop a conscience

- Lying, often for no apparent reason

- Uncertainty about the reliability and predictability of the world

- Problems setting and obeying boundaries

- Social isolation

- Difficulty attuning to other people's emotional states, or a lack of empathy

- Difficulty with understanding others' perspectives

- Inability to self-soothe, i.e., comfort and take care of oneself in a healthy rather than an unhealthy way

Clinically, the picture of the reactive child includes self-destructive behaviors such as the following:

- Eating disorders like anorexia nervosa and bulimia

- Aggression toward both oneself and others

- Pathological self-soothing behaviors including substance abuse and self-mutilation

- Excessive compliance or oppositional-defiant behavior patterns

- Problems associated with understanding or complying with rules

- Low self-esteem

- Shame and guilt

Self-Love

Self-love should not be confused with narcissism. In reality, narcissism is about self-aggrandizement, self-absorption, and treating others as objects. Healthy self-love is about meeting our needs and taking care to not intentionally hurt our self, to be relatively free from chronic internal conflict.

Operationally, self-love implies the healthy ability to take care of one's needs, providing a sense of safety, trust, positive self-worth, and self-regard. Conversely, abuse or violations of the self may logically be seen as anything that violates this operational definition of love or self-love.

As adults, whenever adults subordinate their needs to accommodate another's, which is a typical response style, they violate themselves and lose their integrity. Abused children are typically victims to the will of others. Early-life abuse robs children of a healthy sense of self, depriving them of the ability to feel and experience their own power. As adults, these individuals lack a healthy sense of authority and boundaries. During therapy, and especially therapy regarding the boundary-setting process, I often inform my patients that it is their right to have a right! That revelation frequently reveals the individual's extreme inner doubt about who he or she is and about the individual's self-efficacy or power.

Self-love means self-centeredness in a healthy way—setting the appropriate boundaries to avoid a shame response and benefiting from one's mature interactions with others.

Anne's Story

At fifty-six, Anne sought the services of a life coach to help her deal with her troubled marriage. After two years, her marriage still wasn't improving; so Anne sought the services of a psychotherapist to help her deal with her own issues.

Anne's husband was a police officer, and they had been married for twenty-six years, a first marriage for both. Their marriage had produced three daughters, two of whom continue to live at home. Anne reported that their daughters revealed to her that they felt that home revolves around their father's moods.

When asked about her husband, Anne indicated that he was a very selfish, unhappy man. She said that they had had no sexual intimacy for over a year.

"I'm on guard whenever we go out—I'm afraid he's going to say things about me in public and embarrass me," she said. She appeared withdrawn and unassertive and seemed to be searching for a way of expressing herself that didn't also create more fear for her.

Anne stated her issues as follows:

- "My self-esteem is on the ground. I have no confidence or self-respect. I don't trust myself to defend what I feel or think."

- "I'm codependent. I try to make everybody happy."

- "My mother was critical and very unsupportive."

- "I'm a horrible procrastinator, and I overthink everything."

- "I hate confrontation. Everything was negated by my mother."

- "My husband constantly puts me down. He's even said to me that I don't know what love is."

- "I always worry about someone else first."

Anne was the youngest in a blended marriage. When asked about her relationship with her parents, she said that her mother was twice widowed and now lives two hours away. Her father died when she was quite young, and her mother got remarried. Her new husband was a man who had four children from his previous marriage.

Anne was very forthcoming about her early-life treatment, stating that her mother and stepfather had invalidated her throughout her life with them. Their words still rang in her head, for example, "Anne, that's not very smart." When her therapist asked her how she had dealt with that ongoing derogation, she said, "I began rehearsing everything since I was always waiting for the cut or the dig. I still do all of these things because my mom was such a negative influence, and I still fear being rejected by her."

One of her therapist's first tasks was to have Anne read and understand the nature of boundaries and boundary setting. As Anne began dealing with her shame, she realized that she was living according to her mother's words about her and not her own healthy words about herself. This freed her to deal with her husband in a proactive way. Her codependency began to lift as she negotiated with herself in a healthy, self-supporting way. It was in this way that she found her voice and was able to define with her husband what she would and would not accept from him.

Sexualized Love

Healthy romantic love, with or without sex, is a unique complexity of feelings and characteristically involves feelings of closeness and appreciation. From each new emotional relationship, people frequently learn who they are, gaining new insights and self-knowledge as each relationship provides new experiences within which to learn and grow. As we learned from Harlow's studies with mother surrogates, a human's ability to engage and grow through healthy intimate and romantic adult relationships is most definitely a function of our earliest bonding experiences.

Attachment, on the other hand, provides feelings of safety, comfort, stability, certainty, and empathy. As adults, how we relate with others often directly reflects our earliest bonding experiences. How safe and secure we felt as children directly relates to how we deal with adult relationships, especially the emotions of compassion and empathy toward another. Through healthy communication, we are able to build a bridge toward deep, long-term closeness.

Many adult survivors of childhood abuse, violence, physical and emotional neglect, incest, rape, and molestation frequently confuse sexualized love and romantic love. Frequently called sexual addicts, these individuals, both male and female, have many issues associated with impulsive behavior and confusion as to what love is. Often, their self-acceptance is associated with a sexual response or sexual performance. In the mind and behavior of these individuals, love is highly conditional upon their compulsive needs being met. In sexualized love, the partner is perceived as an object; and if intimacy is present, it is short-lived and usually compartmentalized.

For the sexualized-love addict, the closeness offered by romantic love and healthy sexuality are fraught with conflict in the form of tension, anxiety, and the fear of separation and abandonment. The fear of being alone or rejected propels the individual to seek that "special" relationship, which, if it never materializes, causes these individuals to grow more and more unhappy, fearful, and bored. Out of their fear of being alone and rejected, they typically have multiple relationships of intrigue, flirtations, and affairs that leave a path of destructive relationships and emotional despair.

Similar to drug addicts, sexualized love addicts always seek something outside themselves, either a relationship experience or a physical thing (a new possession such as a car or clothing) to provide them with the stability that they believe they lack. They use their romantic and sexual prowess in an enticing and manipulative attempt to bolster a deflated sense of self and remain emotionally buoyant. Power, manipulation, and control define the sexualized-love addict's relationships. Because the fear of abandonment or rejection is so strong, these codependent relationships are often characterized by overdependence on the partner, shame, and physical and emotional abuse. Often, as a means of coping with the chaotic emotional effects of their own behavior, codependents abuse alcohol and drugs to self-medicate. These compulsive addictive behaviors, though never effective as coping mechanisms, do lower the emotional pain threshold, which helps to deal with the frustrations and emptiness in these individuals' lives.

As we have seen, early-life trauma, abuse, and especially abandonment—either emotional or physical—lead to failures in the development of healthy affects associated with safety, security, affection, empathy, compassion, and trust. As adults, the emotional and psychological toll experienced is great, as is the shame response from ineffective coping mechanisms: violence toward self and others, addictions, compulsive disorders, failures in interpersonal and romantic relationships, chronic mood disorders, and a plethora of other symptoms of shame generally associated with despair, desperation, and emotional isolation.

No matter how many achievements the toxically shamed individual receives or earns, he or she never feels fulfilled or successful. This individual's inner voice always defaults to "I'm not good enough!"

Steven's Story

At forty-two years of age, Steven appeared to have it all. Good looking, with a fine Eastern education and an MBA from a prestigious university, Steven had been married for five years when he presented for treatment. His wife was an attractive forty-seven-year-old and was reported to be rather passive. They had two children, a four-year-old boy and a two-year-old daughter. Steven held a good job, earning a six-figure income as an operations manager for a large American corporation.

When Steven entered therapy, he listed the following observations about himself:

- "I want to control things."
- "I have problems dealing with stress."
- "I'm overwhelmed and overloaded."
- "I don't think I have enough friends."

- "I believe that I have a significant amount of shame."
- "The tape in my head is, 'You're not good enough.'"
- "I have a sense of impending doom."
- "I fear being seen as a fraud."

Despite his outwardly self-confident demeanor, Steven said that he looked at positive feedback from others with skepticism. He sought his validation from work and not from his interpersonal relationships.

Steven's childhood was ridden with painful emotion and insecurity. He was a child of his father's third marriage and had five siblings. He reported that when he was born, his father, a high-ranking civic leader and small business owner, was fifty-five years old and his mother was thirty-two. He wasn't really close to his father, who died at age ninety, and he said that his parents fought his entire life.

"Both my parents were judgmental and hypercritical," Steven remembered. "Most of the time, it was certainly directed at me and was a horrible blow to me because it came from people I trusted."

From an early age, Steven never felt safe. He stated that his father's emotional state ranged through a spectrum of anger, which was highly traumatic for him as a child. "I had a lot of problems at school because of their fighting—it was loud and constant," Steven said.

Steven's father was also homophobic and expressed strong distaste for men who were homosexual.

His parents divorced when Steven was sixteen. He moved

to Florida with his mother, who commenced a life of dating there and married again when Steven was twenty-one. She also spent a lot of time sharing her personal life with Steven in ways that he felt were highly inappropriate, especially when he was a teenager. He added that when he was younger, his mother developed breast cancer and he was obliged to inject her medication.

Steven added that he's not terribly close to his mother. He described her as judgmental and mean-spirited. Steven's feelings regarding his relationship with his mother were expressed in such comments as "My mother is responsible for all the negative things in my head"; "She is super-competitive, and it's hard to trust her"; and "I cannot get close to my mother."

The theme of "lacking confidence" is present in much of what Steven does as well as in reports regarding most aspects of his life. Other than exercising on a very regular basis, Steven has no hobbies and indicates that he never did. "The voice in my head is constantly saying, 'You can't do this,'" he said.

Throughout his early adulthood to the present, Steven reported, "Even though I'm forty-two, I've never felt like an adult;" "Even though I'm married and I should be thinking of my wife's needs first, I save a lot for me and I think of myself first;" and "I just don't feel very good about myself—the fight-or-flight thing is really what I feel, especially at one in the morning."

Through the course of Steven's treatment, he began to realize how distant he had been from his own core of needs and feelings. He also understood how his father's homophobia had further caused Steven's alienation from his own desires.

Steven realized that his needs to be accepted by and to please his parents were the prime reasons that he sought a conventional lifestyle, specifically being married and having a family. He finally concluded that because he had given in to the fear of his parents' abandonment, his true emotional needs were not being met within the confines of his marriage. He had always fought his feelings toward other men; the paralytic shame his father had produced in him caused him to deny his feelings, forcing him to overcompensate by working harder and being more successful. For the first time during his therapy, he was able to experience himself as a "psychological orphan." He was subsequently able to express his feelings openly and allow himself for the first time to explore the possibility of a life of his own choosing.

Steven, with the support and help of his therapist, was able to recognize and accept the fact that living a double life would promulgate more shame and stress, both for himself and his family. For the first time in his relationship with his wife, he elected to openly and honestly share with her who he was and how he felt.

Steven found an apartment close to their home so as to try to minimize the separation effects on their two children. Ultimately divorcing, he reported that for the first time in his life, he felt whole and at peace with himself and no longer experienced the feeling of impending doom. While living openly as a gay man has been a major adjustment for him, he is optimistic about his future.

CHAPTER 6

THE TREATMENT OF SHAME

Only Through Apperception
Can We Truly Know and Heal Our Self

Where Healing Begins

In the treatment of chronic shame and associated shame-based behavior, patients entering treatment for the first time rarely, if ever, speak directly and specifically of shame or especially of their critical self-talk. Rather, the patient may vaguely refer to feelings of worthlessness, being undeserving, or even wondering why he or she is alive at all. Alternatively, individuals who have been through addiction treatment or rehabilitation programs and those in twelve-step programs in which shame is part of the language of recovery can speak more directly to their experiences of shame.

Most of the time, however, new patients refer to general feelings of worthlessness, emptiness, insignificance, depression, or problems "surrounding the wound" but not specifically about their shame experiences. In the early stages of treatment, a therapist looks for or observes the evidence of shame in the patient's associations and may assume the possibility of shame in the presence of defenses that demonstrate that underlying affect. This assumption leads to a search for the possible connections to significant experiences of shame during the patient's childhood. The patient's need to keep his or her sense of defectiveness suppressed or under control often reveals itself in such behaviors as perfectionism, withdrawal, combativeness, obsessive thoughts and behavior, marital and relationship problems, and addictions. Each of these aspects must be addressed; and if addictions are present, they certainly must be addressed first.

As treatment begins, through detailed family history, relational history, and history of trauma and abuse, the patient is able—possibly for the first time and out loud—to recognize and talk about experiences that formed deep and primal shame wounds.

The Difference between Guilt and Shame

Psychoeducationally, I find it effective to differentiate guilt and shame for patients. This way, I am able to facilitate for the patient an understanding of his or her shame defenses as well as the underlying affects and affective responses. By enlisting a patient's support, together we begin the process of searching for connections between the experiences of shame and significant childhood violations that include trauma, abuse, and neglect.

It is critical for therapists to identify or note whether the patient initially trivializes early traumatic events in an effort to suppress or minimalize the pain of those experiences. Indeed, throughout this writing, it has been my attempt to demonstrate that we can look at affects and affective experiences within an empirical framework.

As we can see in Figure 6.1, there is a differentiation between the affective response to shame and the higher-order (cognitive) response of guilt. When a therapist attempts to treat shame wounds within a cognitive-behavioral therapy (CBT) model or approach, what will frequently be missed is the evaluation and tapping of primary affective signatures. As we've seen here, these signatures are the foundation that influence and form an individual's core self and autobiographical self (the self that knows the self through apperception or conscious awareness). For healing to begin, these signatures must be recognized and addressed.

PRIMARY AFFECT ➡ **SHAME**
- Precognitive experiences
- Preverbal experiences
- Does not respond to CBT

SECONDARY EMOTION ➡ **GUILT**
- Cognitive only
- Responds best to CBT

Figure 6.1. Shame and Guilt Responses

When people experience the emotion of guilt, it is usually guilt relating to something they have done or might do: a certain behavior identified as an infraction of their value system. The attendant feeling is usually anxiety, fear, or apprehension. If experienced often, these emotions can become a part of their personality; but they are separate from the person's core self.

In contrast, when people have a shame attack, they experience it in the "core of their being": embarrassing exposure or a painful realization of being seen, a true mortification, a humiliating sense of helplessness and vulnerability, a noncognitive physiological and neurological experience. They don't think about shame; they just feel it. This experience is also unique because it doesn't result from something they intentionally did but rather from their negative reaction to something that was done to them. Without help, they are powerless in the face of it.

Affects and Emotions

Like guilt and shame, affect and emotion are also different. Affect is the precursor of emotion. Damasio (2010) adds scientific credibility in support of this difference, writing that "emotion and feeling have two different faces in keeping with their very different physiological mechanisms" (12–125).

To further the argument that cognitive-behavior therapy is insufficient and fundamentally ineffective in the treatment of shame and negative self-talk, let's look at the three primary assumptions that underscore cognitive-behavioral models of treatment:

- Cognitive processes are accessible and can be known. Although specific thoughts or beliefs may not immediately be apparent to us, patients can become aware of them with proper training and practice.

- Our thinking mediates the way we respond to environmental cues. From the CBT perspective, we do not just react emotionally. Rather, the way we think about our reality is primary to how we react to it.

- Cognition can be intentionally targeted, modified, and changed. Consequently, when such cognitions are changed in the direction of more rational, realistic, and balanced thinking, one's symptoms will be relieved, leading to increased adaptability and functionality (Gonzales-Prendes and Resko, 2012).

As therapists, we know the cognitive-behavioral model to be effective in the treatment of many types of mood and behavioral disorders such as phobias and other symptoms and syndromes associated with thought. But it has been found that there are patients who engage with the cognitive-behavioral tasks of therapy and become skilled at generating alternatives for their negative thoughts and beliefs yet still do poorly in therapy itself (Rector, et al., 2000).

Since shame is affective in nature, the treatment of shame wounds or trauma should be specifically directed not toward thought but the release of affective engrams, the memory traces that shaped and identified us to our self and to the world. Shame cannot be manipulated in the way that cognition or thoughts about our self are treated in cognitive-behavior therapy. As we have seen in earlier chapters, shame wounds and our unique way of dealing with them, including our defenses, reduce our emotional efficacy and block us from apperceiving a healthy image or picture of our self. In essence, shame wounds cause a shutdown in emotional plasticity and relational viability. Thus, unless there is an intervention, we typically continue to reinjure our earlier wound, often throughout our lifetime, without ever believing that there is another way to live and experience our self.

Shame Is a Reaction

It is possible, however, to live a healthy and self-affirming life after a history of abuse, trauma, neglect, chaos, and even a shame-bound existence! From the standpoint of the present model, we can look at shame—and its attendant critical self-talk—not as an immutable disease of our affective development but rather as a *reaction* and a critical voice that can be modified or silenced on several levels. This realization can benefit many traumatized individuals in new and groundbreaking ways.

In my clinical experience with patients who experience chronic and sometimes debilitating shame-core manifestations, a patient's history reveals the etiology of early-life emotional deprivation from absent, abusive, or neglectful parents or care-givers. These individuals' fractured emotional relationships, self-condemnation, and inhibitions reveal deficits in attune-ment, intimacy, and compassion, especially for one's self.

In attempting to identify shame in operational terms for the purposes of treatment, the present model asserts that there are two primary factors associated with shame: *harmonic associations* and *disharmonic associations*.

Harmonic Associations

I define harmonic associations as the dependent variables associated with the treatment of shame based upon therapeutic goals, treatment modalities, and outcomes. Three primary and general treatment goals or outcomes are attunement, empathy, and compassion.

One way to conceptualize the relationship of attunement, empathy, and compassion is in the form of an equation, as laid out in Figure 6.2.

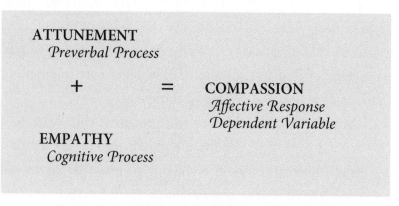

Figure 6.2. A Model of the Compassion Process
How Compassion Happens

Compassion is not a standalone affective response; it is dependent upon the antecedent conditions of both attunement and empathy. Plainly stated, compassion doesn't arise out of the clear blue. In order to experience compassion either for oneself or another, we must be selflessly attuned to the situation and also have a deep understanding of or a connection to another. This must be a central focus and foundation for the therapeutic treatment of shame to occur.

Gilbert (2000) suggests that the ability to experience emotional warmth, to feel reassured, to forgive, and to feel compassion all develop from strategies for forming attachments, friendships, and continuing relationships. Just as we can develop the ability to self-criticize, we can also develop the ability to self-reassure and be compassionate toward the self; the resulting response is most likely one of feeling supported, understood, and cared for. Through the process of apperception, this can be contrasted to the feelings of defeat and submission triggered by self-criticism and attack from self or others.

Disharmonic Associations

I define *disharmonic associations* as the core factors associated with shame. They include:

- Fixation: This describes fractured emotional growth beyond the age at which the trauma, abuse, or neglect began. Shame envelops the area around the wound (trauma) or family processes that established the wound or wounding in the first place.

- Broken attachments: These are effects of a nonnurturing environment, including abusive or absent parents or caregiver(s).

- Fears: Three primary areas of fear in this shame model are abandonment, rejection, and loss of self.

The therapeutic treatment of shame must address each of the three factors associated with disharmonic associations. Of course, therapy cannot in itself create healthy self-worth. Rather, through various approaches that include role-playing, guided imagery, and assertion training, therapists can help their patients relieve and release negative affective associations that have defined them and—most important—maintained and fed their *shame core*. This shame core also includes the ideas of reference that have kept them in a perpetual state of emotional and psychological tyranny, robbing them of healthy defenses and boundaries. They have been prisoners all along!

Shame and Anger

Clinically, shame and anger are actually very closely related. Anger is manifested in many different ways. Very often, therapists may miss essential cues regarding the need to address core issues associated with toxic shame and deal only with the more objective symptoms or personality issues. For example, patients with chronic alcohol or drug addiction may not even present their deeper issues associated with shame, and treatment may address only the cessation of their chemical dependency or abuse.

As we have seen throughout this book, damaging early-life experiences can make one guilty, fearful, suspicious, or filled with rage. These experiences and the manifest ways in which one deals with his or her core issues certainly have an effect on and skew one's perception of self. In treatment, the shame phenomenon requires a special sensitivity on the part of the therapist. As Karen (1992) has stated in this regard, patients might be hypersensitive about acceptance and abandonment and, therefore, uncertain about whether they can trust the therapist with their wound. On the other hand, this is a wound for which they no doubt sense that the therapeutic process has great potential to exacerbate. The therapist must win over the hiding, shameful side of the patient's personality and gradually help it to heal.

Apperception

The notion of apperception is found in the early psychologies of Herbert Spencer, Hermann Lotze, and Wilhelm Wundt circa 1800. Its original meaning was associated with conscious awareness, that is, to perceive; in other words, sensations can break through the limen or threshold into conscious awareness.

In the context of the therapeutic treatment of shame, *apperception* refers to conscious perception with full awareness; that is, the state of the mind being conscious of its own consciousness. Apperception is the process of understanding by which newly observed or experienced qualities of our self are integrated into our associations of past experiences. Most important is the idea that we can communicate or check in with our self. This is a reality that we can use in evaluating our own experiences—a way of self-validation. As a patient of mine stated, "I never understood working on myself. Therapy makes me look at myself." In the direct treatment of shame, the apperception process can:

- Allow patients to discuss, often for the first time, their experience of shame and the toxic aspects of their early-life experiences.

- Detoxify through the discharge of affective energy associated with early wounding.

- Integrate newly experienced affective associations related to one's self in a supportive, protective, and emotionally facilitating environment.

As newly experienced associations pertaining to one's self are introduced and integrated into his or her consciousness, the patient is encouraged to look at and experience his or her self in a self-affirming rather than a self-negating way. It is through the confrontations with parents, siblings, caregivers, or other agents of abuse regarding experiences of shaming (i.e., what they did to me and how I perceived and affectively experienced it) that a patient can begin the integration of healthy adult feelings and self-compassion. This therapeutic process can be as simple as a guided-imagery confrontation with each of the abusers in which the patient verbally and emotionally discharge his or her deepest wounds. In this process, which I believe is very effective, patients are able to release affective energy associated with past experiences in a supportive and safe environment, as adults with an adult "voice" and no longer as helpless child victims.

This process is highly subjective; however, patients begin to truly see themselves differently as they allow themselves to understand that they were not victims of abuse because they were "bad" or defective in some way. In this regard, the patients learn that they are all "perfectly imperfect" (Mellody and Freundlich, 2003, 25-38). Through the process of apperception, patients can look at their shame behavior and defenses in a new light without the affective energy and the defenses that have blocked them, thus having inhibited personal and relational growth.

Through this discharge of affective energy, or *cathexis*,

individuals can begin to understand the nature of their wounding. They can begin the process of owning themselves and developing self-love and self-protection, not through inadequate defenses but through the development of healthy boundaries. They can begin to see their true "self"—not through the screen of scorn, fear, and inadequacy but through the screen of self-love and self-care.

Treatment Processes

Empirically or operationally, compassion training may be seen as a way of teaching or modeling compassionate behavior with the patient. Shame and self-critical thinking are clearly the targets in Compassion-Focused Therapy. Patients often have significant fears related to giving up their negative thinking, as that has been their existing normal. British psychologist Paul Gilbert, proponent of Compassion-Focused Therapy, stated the following:

> Compassion-Focused Therapy is not just about countering threat-based processing or developing different defenses such as learning to be assertive rather than submissive; it also seeks to stimulate positive affect processing. Some clients have developed a fear of enjoying themselves or doing nice things for themselves, and positive emotions can feel threatening because (in part) they are unfamiliar and the individual feels "off guard." Behavioral tasks encouraging exposure to positive emotions can help the client to learn to enjoy experiencing them (2005, 6).

Pia Mellody's Shame-Reduction Treatment Approach

For those experiencing toxic shame, the need to keep one's sense of defectiveness under control or hidden from others often manifests itself as perfectionism, withdrawal, combativeness, anger, obsessive-compulsiveness, or addiction. Certainly, each of these shame aspects must be addressed; however, as noted previously, if any addictions are present, *they must certainly be addressed first before therapy can begin.* Clinicians must be very careful not to trigger the patient's shame core before it has been clinically addressed and treated through measures directly aimed at shame reduction, as with Pia Mellody's approach.

Pia Mellody, the pioneering leader in the treatment of shame through her shame-reduction therapy approach, asserts that patients must release and detoxify both childhood emotions and "carried-feeling reality"; that is, giving back toxic introjects from abusive parents or caregivers and thereby releasing bound-up energy associated with early-life abuse and trauma. For Mellody, early-life trauma, abuse, and neglect are the predetermining factors associated with codependence. Her treatment model appears to have three primary goals for the patient:

- To be less emotionally reactive

- To become more trusting of one's own intuition through becoming the patient's own healthy parent model as well as the repairing of childhood-trauma reactions, leading to a healthy adult state.

- To identify and reduce codependency

Mellody's model and treatment approach were developed

through her attempt to understand her patients with addiction and addictive personalities, including codependence. She believes that shame-based behaviors such as sexual addiction, spousal abuse, and violence are the result of very early exposure to abuse, trauma, and neglect. Her model is outlined in Table 6.1 (Mellody, 2003).

Mellody's treatment approach focuses on shifting the patients from an inhibitory "shutdown" state of shame into the vitality state of assertion and self-care. How is this accomplished? According to her model, through reparenting their self, they take charge of their own wounding and repair it through the release of affective energy. Thus, they take responsibility for their life in the present, moving toward the future. The model stresses that patients must learn to accept the fact that they are not perfect and that perfection is not a possible or realistic goal to achieve; that is, they must learn to accept their perfectly imperfect self. The goal of Mellody's model is to become a more "functional adult," one who is able to display righteous anger that releases the affects and allows for healthy self-assertive behavior to develop.

Much of Mellody's theory is based upon many assumptions and anecdotal records gathered from her own early-life trauma and abuse as well as from her patients' experiences. However, from an empirical standpoint, one important set of dependent variables associated with her theory of shame attacks (although she has only minimally discussed it) may be seen as critical to the measurement and treatment of shame.

Table 6.1. Pia Mellody's Post-Induction Therapy Model

Somatic experiencing is sensing one's body state and also feeling one's emotional reactions in a given situation. This technique is used in the treatment of post-traumatic stress.

Guided imagery is utilized to confront the family of origin and other violators. Violators may also be confronted verbally

Boundary setting, which comprises physical, sexual, emotional, and spiritual areas of one's life.

Assertion training means learning how to stand up, speak out, and talk back without the experience of shame. It is the process of applying boundaries that establish one's positive sense of self as a healthy adult.

Post-traumatic stress-reduction therapy, including stress inoculation and relaxation training, is utilized to increase one's threshold for frustration tolerance and learning to keep expectations of one's self and others realistic

Medical intervention and stabilization are necessary for chemical dependency, substance abuse, and alcoholism. Family treatment is also a primary feature of Mellody's program.

These are the dimensions of:

- Frequency

- Intensity

- Duration

By monitoring the frequency, intensity, and duration of shame attacks and the chatter of critical self-talk that accompanies them, patients can continue their emotional and spiritual development as "functional adults" while preserving and protecting their inner child. If these three variables are monitored throughout the therapy process and after, it can provide, at the least, a subjective measure of a patient's self-growth in dealing with shame and its behavioral manifestations. This includes shame-based behavior, alcohol and substance addiction, domestic violence, and PTSD.

Developing Trust

Another primary outcome of therapy—possibly less measurable but central to emotional and relational health—is a less reactive and more trusting change in attitude and behavior both of self and others. When early bonding is shattered or nonexistent, healthy patterns of trust may not develop either affectively or neurologically. When a nonnurturing parent or caregiver is cold or punitive, the child's "alarm system" will constantly provide signals to the brain (fight or flight) that he or she isn't safe. This prompts the use of primitive defenses to protect—not soothe—one's self, thus creating a sense of *never really feeling safe.*

When children expect derogation—or worse, when they know that they do not matter—their sense of self will be hypersensitive to negative stimuli. The therapeutic development of trust is of major importance to the successful outcome of treatment. Trusting one's own intuition is a corollary of trust itself. When patients begin to truly trust their self, we also begin to trust the intuitive, affective nonverbal aspect of our experiencing and perception.

We might ask this question: What about the preverbal or nonconscious aspect of shame? As we have seen in earlier chapters, it has been hypothesized (Damasio, 1999, 2010) that trauma experienced prior to self or self-awareness is stored in the basal ganglia of the brain and is there to influence us in many different ways. These toxic experiences or exposures associated with neglect, violence, abuse of any kind, or threats to self will produce the behavioral and emotional characteristics of *trauma*.

SAMHSA

The Substance Abuse and Mental Health Services Administration (SAMHSA) is the agency within the U.S. Department of Health and Human Services that leads public-health efforts to advance the behavioral health of the nation. SAMHSA's mission is to reduce the impact of substance abuse and mental illness on America's communities.

Nationally recognized professional associations, family and consumer/peer-specialist groups, research and practice entities, and diagnostic and medical groups have endorsed differing definitions of trauma. After extensive review and discussion of these various definitions, the following working definition of individual trauma was developed by SAMHSA:

> Individual trauma results from an event, series of events, or set of circumstances that is experienced by an individual as physically or emotionally harmful or threatening and that has lasting adverse effects on the individual's functioning and physical, social, emotional, or spiritual well-being (SAMHSA, 2014, 7).

In other words, *events and circumstances* may include the actual or extreme threat of physical or psychological harm or the withholding of material or relational resources essential to healthy development. These events and circumstances may occur once or repeatedly over time:

> The individual's experience of these events or circumstances helps to determine whether it is a traumatic event. A particular event may be experienced as traumatic for one individual and not for another. For example: One child removed from an abusive home may experience this as traumatic, whereas another may not; one refugee may experience fleeing one's country as traumatic, another may not; one military veteran may experience deployment to a war zone as traumatic, another may simply take this in stride. How the individual labels and assigns meaning to any event and how he or she is disrupted physically and psychologically by it will determine whether it is experienced as traumatic.

> In many situations, a sense of humiliation, betrayal, or silencing often shapes the experience of the event.

How the event is experienced may be linked to a range of factors, including the individual's cultural beliefs (e.g., the subjugation of women and the experience of domestic violence), availability of social supports (whether isolated or embedded in a supportive family or community structure), or to the developmental stage of the individual (i.e., an individual may understand and experience events differently at age five, fifteen or fifty) (Wilson, C. and Ford, J. 2012, 1).

In a recent study evaluating the role of shame and self-critical thinking (self-talk) with regard to post-traumatic stress disorder (PTSD), Harman and Lee (2010) found that individuals with PTSD who reported higher levels of shame were more prone to engage in self-critical thinking and less prone to engage in self-reassuring thinking than those with PTSD who reported lower levels of shame. These researchers suggest that therapy for shame-based PTSD needs to incorporate strategies to help individuals develop inner caring, compassion, and self-reassurance (Harman and Lee, 2010, 13).

Trauma and the effects of early-life abuse and neglect often result clinically in heightened states of arousal and vigilance, with low frustration tolerance in many adults. Very often, we see patients who are highly reactive. This heightened reactivity has been attributed to a highly sensitized reticular activating system and corresponding levels of vigilance and hypervigilance. In our patients, we often see the results of early-life abuse and neglect as characterized by dysfunctional and self-defeating behaviors as well as poor coping skills attributable to low thresholds for frustration. These patients often respond well to relaxation training, hypnosis, guided imagery, and other somatic therapies.

Compassion

Compassion is a spontaneous sensory experience that triggers a deep, harmonic autonomic affective response. The role of compassion cannot be overstated in its importance for overcoming the effects of early-life abuse and toxic shame. Victims of such abuse often lack compassion, both for self and others. The healing properties of compassion have been written about for centuries. The Dalai Lama (2001) has often stressed that if you want others to be happy, you should focus on compassion, but if you want to be happy yourself, you should still focus on compassion.

Compassion has no voice; it just is (or isn't). Compassion is a feeling toward another and is not an emotion. Compassion is a connectedness that transcends language and emotion. Compassion is preverbal and spontaneous.

Have you ever come across that one animal in a shelter whose situation suddenly speaks to you of all animals, or listened to someone relating a personal experience of loss or tragedy and you suddenly have a physiological feeling of connection? Sometimes, a patient will be relating a historical or recent aspect of his or her experience, and I will experience goose bumps, an autonomic reaction that I have come to recognize as a compassionate response. I cannot control it—it's not intellectual. It is a deep connection of an association with the other.

Unlike empathy, which is an "understanding" that requires thought and is most often conveyed through language toward and with another through our own life experiences, compassion is an affective response developed (or not developed) through our earliest experiences. As we have seen, healthy infant bonding helps to ensure the healthy development of safety, trust, and affection in adulthood. With unhealthy or broken attachments, what gets lost over time is the bond with our self. The self gets lost and stuck in the quagmire of our toxic life experiences. We become disenfranchised from our being, or who we are at the core.

Self-Compassion

By its very nature, compassion is not limited to our experience with another. We can, and hopefully will, also experience self-compassion. At the center of treatment for toxic shame and negative self-evaluation and self-harm is the absolute necessity for self-compassion. Quite possibly, no treatment approach and focus are more important than Compassion-Focused Therapy. Self-compassion means forgiving our self for sins we did not commit. It means learning how to stop carrying shame, the shame perpetrated by those who violated us in the first place— those who directly or indirectly told us that we were not good enough through their words or actions. Its end result was a violation of our sense of safety, well-being, and self-worth.

When we speak of compassion, I believe we are in effect, referring to self-compassion. Functionally, we need to have self-compassion before we can know how to or be able to have compassion for another. A patient must be encouraged to view the self as a viable and relational aspect of his or her own person. Through the therapeutic process, we can learn to check in and connect with our self.

Compassion, when not present in early nurturing or care-giving experiences, creates within children a sense of fearful-ness and worthlessness. Their wants and needs don't matter. Their world is seen as threatening and non-supportive, with the potential for violence and chaos always looming. These children never feel safe. All roads lead to the feared abandonment. To these individuals, the world feels cold and unsafe. The wounds of early-life abuse are never forgotten!

Compassion-Focused Therapy: The Therapist's Role as a Model

Critical within the scope of therapy is the relationship between the patient and therapist. Trust is essential, but more important is the discussion of trust—what trust means and where it did or did not exist in the patient's early development and relationship with caregivers.

Thus, the objective of Compassion-Focused Therapy is the introduction of a kind and forgiving self. Because we have consciousness and awareness, we do have easy access to the self despite the seeming loss of healthy self. But we can learn to have a dialogue with our self. We can learn to set healthy bound-aries with it. Most important, we have the capacity to develop compassion for our self so we can begin to heal our wounds and protect our self from creating new wounds.

The therapist must model compassion for the patient to make it real. For example, mindfulness, hypnosis, and guided imagery are helpful therapeutic methods of assisting the patient in dialoguing with his or her compassionate self and quieting the inner critic.

John's Story

John is a forty-nine-year-old artist and designer whose self-loathing was so intense that it drove him from one toxic relationship to another. He entered treatment at age forty-four after the death of his father, presenting with avoidance and extreme distrust of people in general. "I don't want people to have any access to me" and "I've become very paranoid—everything I see is laced with motive" were statements representative of his state of self. He also self-described a sense of violence in himself early in his therapy, saying that he'd always had a "violent streak." John's therapist quickly realized that John had a rage disorder.

On the other hand, John was non-assertive and feared telling people who he was and what he wanted. He was even afraid to ask people for money borrowed from him, fearing their reactions if he asked for what was rightfully his. In that regard, he stated, "The only skill I have for dealing with my conflicts is to run away. I avoid, I sacrifice. My whole reality is built around avoidance. Anytime I stand up for myself, I feel guilty."

Somewhere between ages four and seven, John had

developed an awareness of not liking himself. When he entered therapy, however, he had enough understanding of himself to admit that it this behavior was no longer working for him.

As the oldest son of an abusive and frequently absent pilot father and a passive, codependent mother, John knew at an early age that he was "different." John was, in fact, gay, and that was unacceptable to his macho father. No matter how much John achieved professionally, he never felt accepted, either by himself or others. Always fearing rejection, he picked partners who were emotionally absent and avoidant.

Alcohol and marijuana became John's constant companions and support system. He wasn't a heavy drinker, but he had an addiction to marijuana and smoked pot daily. He stated that he experienced insomnia if he didn't smoke pot. It also helped soothe his loneliness. As far as faith or spiritualism went, John didn't subscribe to any beliefs or belief systems.

John's parents had divorced when he was fifteen years old. John's mother was passively codependent with regard to her husband. "My mother always operated out of fear, and I've always operated out of fear," John said. "As a child, I never felt protected or safe."

When his father wasn't ignoring his son completely, he'd treat him with complete disdain. John's self-talk that his father had ingrained in his psyche included "You're a bum, a loser, a fag." "I knew exactly what he thought of me," John said. "I grew up being indicted and convicted before the trial."

During the course of treatment, John described a memory that had suddenly popped into his brain. Somewhere between ages ten and twelve, he and his father went into the forest by their home to chop wood. "I was alone with [my father] all day long, and it was a day of abuse," John said.

John remembered that it was freezing outside and he was in pain from the cold. He said that he felt degraded the entire time, and he revealed that he truly believed his father was going to kill him that day in the woods.

After approximately six months of treatment focusing on developing a relationship with his therapist and providing a level of acceptance he'd never experienced, John said, "I'm starting to recognize all my bullshit, and I'm really becoming aware of how much I'm addicted to stress. I have no inventory of positive experiences about myself—only negative ones. As a child, I'd never asked for anything because it would just cause a fight. I've always had a desperate need for acceptance and attention—I'm always apologizing for myself. My recollection of my childhood was that I did nothing right. Even my creativity always had a caveat."

Since the sense of rejection had been the primary theme in John's early-life history and was the cause of his being highly avoidant, John equated being alone with being rejected.

As his treatment continued, John was beginning to not have "bad weeks" anymore. At one point, he noted that he realized how "visceral and primal" his defensive responses were, meaning the automatic nature of his reactions and his inability to reflect upon his own sense of self in a non-self-abusive way.

"I have consciousnesses at the same time, and I am beginning to notice avoidant behavior that feels wired within me,"

John said. "I'm also aware of my inability to talk about myself in the first-person-present time. All I see is this avoidance that goes on and on."

Toward the end of treatment, John reported a rise in his self-respect. "I can see me being me," he said. "Respect is at the center of it all."

Tapping the Shame Core

It is my belief that unless the shame core associated with early-life trauma, abuse, neglect, abandonment, or violation of any kind is "tapped"—or reexperienced and exposed in a controlled, therapeutic environment—and the affective energy associated with core experiences is released to see the light of day (that is, verbalized, felt, and cathected), *no therapeutic approach will have lasting effects toward the reduction or elimination of toxic shame.* New learning cannot occur regarding self-growth and self-understanding unless this happens.

Many patients drop out of therapy prematurely, often in despair, because the shame aspect of their symptoms was never addressed; or worse, cognitive-behavioral methods were employed to reduce or extinguish the negative self-talk associated with shame. And that is a shame!

Not all treatment or healing of shame happens in a therapeutic or clinical setting. Robert Karen (1992) asserts that life experience in the form of observation, accomplishment, and confrontation with one's self can over time help resolve negative self-views. Additionally, when we are in a relationship wherein each person feels free to explore aspects of the self (which are normally closely guarded) and can express painful early-life experiences, we grow and are able to open up a previously closed system. Additionally, allowing our self to put shame into words with a trusted companion enables one to step outside it. In so doing, shame no longer seems to permeate our entire being, and self-forgiveness can finally emerge. Through the process of self-forgiveness, we begin to heal the wounds inflicted by early caregivers, which we assumed we created ourselves and continued to punish ourselves for through our toxic self-talk and shame-based behaviors.

The mental, emotional, and relational costs associated with keeping shame in the closet can be horrific. Shame frequently propels human beings into a busy, outwardly directed life in which the last person on earth they wish to know is their self! What could be worse than that?

For the most part, writing about shame has primarily been associated with twelve-step and recovery programs. Because of its name and its very nature or what it implies and its universality, shame has not been popularized in clinical or empirical literature to any extent. Yet with regard to our understanding of shame as a bio/psycho/social component of our self, it appears to be the elephant in the corner of the consulting room that nobody wants to look at! This book has been an attempt to not only look at the elephant but to in fact understand it and start to tame it, and this is both critically important and possible.

It is my hope that through the effective treatment of toxic shame, patients can become less conflicted as healthy adults, and partner with and allow their internal child to freely and spon-taneously roam in safety throughout their life. Through this process, they can ultimately find their true, essential, and healthy inner voice.

AFTERWORD

In many families, unprocessed trauma and shame in the form of addiction are handed down from a parent or caregiver to the infant or child in the form of emotional distance or neglect, distrust and a lack of authenticity. Clinically, what we see in these children is often some degree of pervasive sadness, anger, depression, or the admixture of all three. It is sometimes expressed as "poor me." When these children are bullied, as they often are, their emotional reactions turn to blind rage—a rage so violent and horrific that the consequences are all too often unimaginable.

In recent times, our country has been rocked by the growing incidence of shootings at schools and in other public areas, committed primarily by males in their teens and early twenties. Going from theory to reality, the profiles of these school shooters all share certain characteristics: no bonding, or broken bonds; disenfranchisement and alienation from family and peers; and a lot of harbored anger and rage of the kind that identifies everyone else as the source of their misery. They are loners and emotionally isolated, with no healthy way to diffuse their internal rage. This rage is born of a loss of self and self-worth as well as the inability to understand compassion and its antecedents, empathy and attunement, especially for self or others. These kids also lack the capacity or ability to self-soothe and typically show no remorse for their horrific acts, that is if they survive; most don't.

This understanding must be more than a wake-up call. There needs to be both a national and an international movement to do more than simply study the problem. We need cooperation at the local and national levels to protect innocents from such terror. We must have better tools to identify those at high risk, and we also need appropriate and immediate interventions in order to stem the tide of toxic shame and violence that has caused so much unnecessary loss of life and suffering.

It is my sincere hope that for the reader, the benefit and meaning of this book derive from the theoretical and empirical understanding of toxic shame and its sequelae as formulated here. What I believe to be yet more important is the practical application to the prevention and treatment of toxic shame.

GERALD LOREN FISHKIN, PH.D.
LOS ANGELES, CALIFORNIA

APPENDIX A:
AFFIRMING ISN'T LEARNING

The thing about affirmations is this: While they are or can be temporarily soothing, they are palliative at best. Affirmations do not change learned behavior in the long run. Like platitudes, they're general and superficial; and they march people into a state of false empowerment. They are just a temporary fix without long-term results.

Affirmations are redundant perceived truths claiming to ameliorate everything from allergies and acne to marital problems. They are a cover-up. True emotional change is affective in nature, arising from and influencing feelings. Everything else is overcompensation or a denial set.

Affirmations can have a parochial foundation and provide a spiritual connection for some. However, we will not find the nexus, the connection to our primordial issues, by affirming them away. It is impossible to connect those dots through positive affirmation. The more painful outcome of relying on affirmations is deferring a truer understanding of our self for a quick fix that has no staying power.

Affirmations will especially not change negative self-talk. How can they? Give it a try. We could call this the ventriloquist principle—but who's the master and who's the dummy? But at the end of the day, negative self-talk doesn't change behavior. It only stirs our feelings up, leaving us back to where we started—feeling bad about our self, feeling shame.

The only time children affirm is when they are forced to repeat something, like writing one hundred times something they'll never do again. These affirmations are called standards, and they don't change anything. Often, these standards simply make the child angrier, not different. Standards usually satisfy an adult's need to feel effective and in control. But the child's behavior does not change as a function of this compulsive and ineffective ritual. In the same way, adult standards/affirmations are redundant and do not change self-critical thoughts or treat the core shame wounds.

Appendix B
Maria's Story

I once heard Oprah say that all everyone really wanted was to know that they matter, to be acknowledged, and to feel validated. Going to therapy has helped me to feel validated and to know that I am not alone in having survived the chaos of abuse and neglect. Nor am I alone in my desire to heal, get better, and go about the business of living a healthy and happy life.

Things happen for a reason and with divine timing, and most of the time we don't even realize the magnitude of life-changing events and how and when they happen until we're far enough ahead of them to look back and see things as they really were. I feel as if it were meant to be that I started going to therapy when and with whom I did. I know I wouldn't have gained as much from it years ago as I have now. I wouldn't have been able at that time to be open enough to understand everything and finally heal. Well, actually, I had no idea how much I even needed to go to therapy years ago. To really tell the truth, I wouldn't have gone at all years ago!

Now, at this time in my life, I can understand and see why I felt so much shame when my ex-husband divorced me. At the time, of course, I felt devastated, sad, and angry; but more than all that, I felt so ashamed. I also remember wondering why phobias, fears, and bad memories that I thought were behind me suddenly seemed to be back in full force and so unmanageable, as if I were coming undone. I discovered that it's because I was coming undone. I was unraveling at the seams, or at least the facade I had been keeping up was unraveling. I thought I had it all together. I thought I had my life so in order that the shame of feeling abandoned, abused, and neglected would all just go away; or at least disappear while I kept a tight lid on it all. The tight lid showed up in the form of me being in control of my life and trying to be perfect, e.g., being in the National Guard and working my way through college, having a big house in the suburbs that was always immaculate, working in a prestigious job with a lot of responsibility, and being in a seemingly great marriage with a man who claimed to "worship the ground I walked on." Even that supposed term of endearment is very telling, now that I think about it, of just how perfect I was trying to be. So when the ex-husband said he wasn't in love with me anymore, it was the straw on the proverbial camel's back. I would not be betrayed, abandoned, and unloved by someone who was supposed to always be there for me and hold the lid on all that shame at the same time. So everything I hadn't dealt with from my childhood came rushing back tenfold. No wonder the pain and sadness as well as feelings of unworthiness and shame felt unbearable.

So what did I do? Did I make the connections and seek the help of a professional? I was far too wounded and ashamed for that, so I ran. I ran away to California and I gave up everything that had failed to help me hide all the pain from the past. I moved here, and I tried to act like I didn't see the open wound. When the wound starting bleeding, I put Band-Aids on it. When it started oozing, I tried to numb it with drugs and disinfect it with alcohol. All the self-medicating in the world couldn't make it go away. In fact, the open wound got infected; and the anger, shame, and pain had to get worse before it could ever begin to get better. What I would metaphorically equate with scraping the wound out deeply enough to cry out in pain was the realization that from the second I came into this world, I had a shame-filled life.

The shame I felt after getting divorced was just the tip of the iceberg. The woman who gave birth to me had been full of shame before I was born in the middle of the night while she was alone in her bedroom in her parents' house. She felt even more shame at having a biracial child and no husband, and she conveniently placed it all upon me. I had a mother who was so disconnected from me that I was emotionally abandoned at conception, which added layer upon complicated layer of pain and more shame to my chaotic childhood spent with her and the monster she later married.

Thank God I started to realize that since I made it out of my childhood alive, I'm a survivor and not a victim. I began to get it together and understand how everything happens for a reason. Then, I had to go through the shame and sadness of my divorce in order to heal from the shame and sadness I felt as a child. (I should write my ex-husband a thank-you note, but I won't.) Back to how everything happens for a reason—I know that I had to go through all of that so that the wound really could be wide open. I had to learn not to be so afraid of all that pain and to face it. Therapy allowed me to do that. I really do believe that now that all the poison is out, I can heal. I'm sewing up the wound, and I'm not looking back.

BIBLIOGRAPHY

Affect. *n.d.*. In *Merriam-Webster Online Dictionary*.
http://www.merriam-webster.com/dictionary/affect

Allport, G. W. 1955. *Becoming*. New Haven: Yale University
Press.

Andreas, S. 2012. *Transforming negative self-talk*. New York:
W. W. Norton and Company.

Bechara, A., A. R. Damasio, H. Damasio, T. J. Grabowski, R. D.
Hichwa, J. Parvizi, and L. L. B. Ponto. 2000. "Subcortical
and cortical brain activity during the feeling of self-
generated emotions." *Nature Neuroscience*, 3(10), 1049–
1056.

Beck, A. T., and B. A. Alford. 2009. *Depression, causes and
treatment*. Philadelphia: University of Pennsylvania Press.

Beckert-Weidman, A., L. Ehrmann, and D. H. LeBow. 2012.
The attachment therapy companion. New York. W. W.
Norton and Company.

Bloom, B. S. 1956. *Taxonomy of Educational Objectives,
Handbook 1: The Cognitive Domain*. New York: David
McKay Co., Inc.

Bradshaw, J. 1988. *Healing the shame that binds*. Deerfield
Beach, FL: Health Communications, Inc.

Branford, J. D., A. L. Brown, and R. R. Cockling, eds. 1999.
How people learn: Brain, mind, experience, and school.
Washington, DC: National Academy Press.

Clark, Don. 2005. "Bloom's taxonomy of learning domains" *Big Dog and Little Dog's Performance Juxtaposition.* http://www.nwlink.com/~donclark/hrd/bloom.html

Dalai Lama. 2001. *Ethics for the new millennium.* New York, NY: The Penguin Publishing Company.

Dalton, L. 2005. "Oxytocin. List of Top Pharmaceuticals." *Chemical and Engineering News,* 83(25). https://pubs.acs.org/cen/coverstory/83/8325/8325oxytocin.html

Damasio, A. 1999. *The feeling of what happens.* Orlando, FL: Harcourt, Inc.

Damasio, A. 2010. *Self comes to mind.* New York, NY: Pantheon Books.

Dennett, Daniel. n.d.. *The normal well-tempered mind.* http://edge.org/conversation/the-normal-well-tempered-mind.

DiCiacco, J. A. 2007 *Attachment disorders.* Buffalo, New York: CMI Education Institute, Inc.

Erikson, E. H. 1950. *Childhood and Society.* New York, NY: Norton.

Erikson, E. H. 1958. *Young Man Luther.* New York, NY: Norton.

Erikson, E. H. 1964. *Insight and Responsibility.* New York, NY: Norton.

Erikson, E. H. 1968. *Identity: Youth and Crisis.* New York, NY: Norton.

Firestone, R. W., L. Firestone, and J. Catlett. 2002. *Conquer Your Critical Inner Voice.* Oakland, CA: New Harbinger Press, Inc.

Ford, J. and C. Wilson. 2012. SAMHSA's trauma and trauma-informed care experts meeting. Cited in Substance Abuse and Mental Health Services Administration. *SAMHSA's Concept of Trauma and Guidance for a Trauma-Informed Approach*. HHS Publications No. (SMA) 14-4884. Rockville, MD: Substance Abuse and Mental Health Services Administration, 2014.

Forsling, M. L. 2001. "Oxytocin." In *The Oxford Companion to the Body*, edited by C. Blakemore and S. Jennet. http://www.encyclopedia.com/topic/oxytocin.aspx#1

Fossum, M. and M. Mason. 1986. *Facing Shame: Families in Recovery*. New York, NY: W. W. Norton and Company, Inc.

Freeman, W. 1995. *Societies of Brains*. Hillsdale, N.J.: Lawrence-Erlbaum Associates.

Freeman, W. 1999. *How Brains Make Up Their Minds*. London, England: Weldenfel and Nicolson.

Gilbert, P. 2000. "Social mentalities: Internal 'social' conflicts and the role of inner warmth and compassion in cognitive therapy." In *Genes on the Couch: Explorations in Evolutionary Psychotherapy*, edited by P. Gilbert and K. G. Bailey, 118–150. Hove, UK: Psychology Press.

Gilbert, P. 2003. "Evolution, social roles, and the differences in shame and guilt." *Social Research* 70: 1205–1230.

Gilbert, P. ed. 2005. *Compassion: Conceptualisations, Research and use in Psychotherapy*. New York, NY: Routledge.

Gilbert, P., and M. T. McGuire. 1998. "Shame, status, and social roles: Psychobiology and evolution." In *Shame: Interpersonal Behaviour, Psychopathology, and Culture*, edited by I. P. Gilbert and B. Andrews, 99–125. New York, NY: Oxford University Press.

Gonzales-Prendes, A. A., and S. M. Resko. 2012. "Cognitive-behavioral theory." In *Trauma: Contemporary Directions in Theory, Practice, and Research,* edited by S. Ringel and J. Brandell, 14–40. Los Angeles, CA: Sage Publications, Inc.

Griffiths, P. E. 1997. *What Emotions Really Are: The Problem of Psychological Categories.* Chicago: The University of Chicago Press.

Harman, R., and D. Lee. 2010. "The role of shame and self-critical thinking in the development and maintenance of current threat in post-traumatic stress disorder." *Clinical Psychology Psychotherapy.* Jan.–Feb., 17(1): 13–24.

Harlow, H. F. 1958. "The nature of love." *American Psychologist,* 13(12): 673–685.

Holohan, M. 2013. "Unborn babies are hearing you, loud and clear" *Today Parents,* August 26. http://www.today.com/parents/unborn-babies-are-hearing-you-loud-clear-8C11005474

James, W. 1890. *The Principles of Psychology.* New York, NY: Henry Holt and Co.

Karen, R. 1992. "Shame". *The Atlantic Monthly,* 269(2): 40–70

Kaufman, G. 1974. "The meaning of shame: Toward a self-affirming identity." *Journal of Consulting Psychology,* 21(9): 568–574.

Krathwohl, D. R., B. S. Bloom, and B. B. Masia. 1973. *Taxonomy of educational objectives: The classification of educational goals, Handbook 11: Affective Domain.* New York, NY: David McKay Co., Inc.

Lane, R., E. M. Reiman, G. L. Ahern, G. E. Schwartz, and R .J. Davidson. 1997. "Neuroanatomical correlates of happiness, sadness, and disgust." *American Journal of Psychiatry,* 154: 926–933.

Learning, medical definition. *n.d.* In *Merriam-Webster Online Dictionary.*
http://www.merriam-webster.com/medical/learning

Levine, A. and M. A. Heller. 2010 *Attached: The New Science of Adult Attachment and How It Can Help You Find—and Keep—Love.* New York, NY: Penguin Group.

Lewis, M. 1992. *Shame: The exposed self.* New York, NY: The Free Press.

Matos, M., and J. Pinto-Gouveia. 2010. "Shame as a traumatic memory." *Clinical Psychology and Psychotherapy*, 17: 299–312.

Mellody, P. 1989. *Facing Codependence.* New York, NY: Harper Collins.

Mellody, P. 2003. "Post-induction therapy training model for developmental maturity." Unpublished training manual. The Meadows, Wickenburg, AZ.

Mellody, P. and L. Freundlich. 2003. *The intimacy factor.* New York, NY: HarperCollins.

Moberg, K. U. 2003. *The Oxytocin Factor: Tapping the Hormone of Calm, Love, and Healing.* Cambridge, MA: Da Capo Press.

Mosby's Medical Dictionary, 9th ed. 2013. Philadelphia, PA: Elsevier Inc.

Nathanson, D. L. 1994. *Shame and Pride: Affect, Sex and the Birth of the Self.* New York, NY: W. W. Norton and Company.

Nicolosi, J. 2009. "The power of therapeutic attunement." http://www.josephnicolosi.com/the-power-of -therapeutic-attun/

Overbaugh, R. C. and L. Schultz. *n.d. New version of Bloom's Taxonomy. Bloom's Taxonomy.* Norfolk, VA: Old Dominion University.

Picard, R. W., S. Papert, W. Bender, B. Blumberg, C. Breazeal, D. Cavallo, T. Machover, M. Resnick, D. Roy and C. Strohecker. 2004. "Affective learning—A manifesto." *BT Technology Journal*, 22(4): October.

Potter-Efron, R., and P. Potter-Efron. 1989. *Letting Go of Shame: Understanding How Shame Affects your Life.* Center City, Minnesota: Hazelden.

Psychology Today, n.d. Psych basics: Guilt. http://www.psychologytoday.com/basics/guilt

Rector, N. A., R. M. Bagby, Z. V. Segal, R. T. Joffe, and A. Levitt. 2000. "Self-criticism and dependency in depressed patients treated with cognitive therapy or pharmacotherapy." *Cognitive Therapy and Research*, 24: 571–584.

Ruiz, D. M. and D. J. Ruiz. 2010. *The Fifth Agreement.* San Rafael, CA: Amber-Allen Publishing, Inc.

Sander, L. W. 2002. "Thinking differently: Principles of process in living systems and the specificity of being known." *Psychoanalytic Dialogues*, 112(1): 11–42.

Schore, A. 2003. *Affect Regulation and the Repair of the Self.* New York, NY: Norton.

Simpson E. J. 1972. *The Classification of Educational Objectives in the Psychomotor Domain.* Washington, DC: Gryphon House.

Smilkstein, R. 2003. *We're Born to Learn.* Thousand Oaks, CA: Corwin Press

Substance Abuse and Mental Health Services Administration, Trauma and Justice Strategic Initiative. 2012. *SAMHSA's working definition of trauma and guidance for trauma-informed approach*. Rockville, MD: Substance Abuse and Mental Health Services Administration.

Tangney, J. P. 1995. "Recent advances in the empirical study of shame and guilt." *American Behavioral Science*, 38: 1132–1145.

Tangney, J. P., and R. L. Dearing. 2002. *Shame and Guilt*. New York, NY: The Guilford Press.

Tomkins, S. S. 1963. *Affect, Imagery, and Consciousness*, Vol. 2. New York, NY: Springer and Co.

VandenBos, G. R., ed. 2006. *APA Dictionary of Psychology*. Washington, DC: American Psychological Association.

Welwood, J. 2000. *Toward a Psychology of Awakening*. Boston, MA: Shambala Publications, Inc.

Wilson, C. and J. Ford. 2012. SAMHSA's Trauma and Trauma-Informed Care Experts Meeting.

Zemak-Rugar, Y, J. R. Bettman, and G. J. Fitzsimmons. 2007, "The effects of nonconsciously priming emotion concepts on behavior." *Journal of Personality and Social Psychology*, 93(1): 927–939.

INDEX

Other Books by Dr. Gerald Loren Fishkin:

American Dream American Burnout
Police Burnout
Firefighter and Paramedic Burnout

Please take some time to visit:

www.drgeraldfishkin.com
www.parkhurstbrothers.com

Psychology / Personal Growth

How to see life as a challenge, not a chore

This book was written for anyone who wants to be free from the tyranny of stress and burnout. Burnout can affect anyone, especially in today's world, where "The American Dream" has been replaced by the realities of a faltering economy, breakdown of the family and societal distintegration. Burnout is not a natural state, and no one should have to live with its emotional pain. Dr. Fishkin explains how to readjust couterproductive thought processes and behaviors and learn new, healthy methods for coping. He details both self-help techniques and suggested resources to reach out to the community or the workplace for assistance.

Paperback • $16.95 • 978-1-62491-077-7
168 Pages @ 7" x 8.5"

Previously Published

Now available through
Parkhurst Brothers Publishers.

"Among the hundred of cases I see every year, burnout is a surprisingly common thread. Dr. Fishkin has written the definitive book on overcoming burnout."
—Arnold Fox, MD, author, *The Beverly Hills Diet*

2016 Author Tour
Radio Promotion

"This book outlines the dangers of worshipping the trapping of societal success, and challenges us to redefine ourselves in ways that support a better sense of show we are. It insightfully explores the attitudes and values that undermine our well being and provides a valuable guide from the stress and unrealistic expectations that binds our creative spirit."
—Ronald Wong Jue, PhD, past president, Association for Transpersonal Psychology

Gerald Loren Fishkin, PhD, author, lecturer and psychotherapist, is an internationally recognized authority on stress and burnout. Dr. Fishkin holds a doctorate in clinical psychology. His theories are based not only on scientific fact and current research, but on his years of experience as a treating clinician. Dr. Fishkin has been in practice since 1970.

PARKHURST
BROTHERS
PUBLISHERS

To Order: 800-621-2736 • www.parkhurstbrothers.com • All major distributors

Psychology / Police

The whip that drives us is held by our own hand

Police Burnout is the synthesis of Dr. Fishkin's sixteen years experience as a police psychologist, and is a must read for all police officers, family members, police and public safety administrators, as well as mental health specialists who work in the area of law enforcement. It is a modern classic in the field of police psychology.

Paperback • $17.95 • 978-1-62491-078-4
248 Pages @ 5" x 8"

Previously Published by Harcourt Brace Jovanovich Legal and Professional Publications, Inc.

Now available through Parkhurst Brothers Publishers.

2016 Author Tour
Radio Promotion

Table of Contents

Chapter 1   The Dynamics of Police Stress

Chapter 2   Dealing Effectively with Police Stress

Chapter 3   Anxiety

Chapter 4   Depression

Chapter 5   Crisis—The Sequence and Response

Chapter 6   Police Burnout—An Operational Definition

Chapter 7   Alcoholism and the Police Officer

Chapter 8   Post-Shooting Trauma

Chapter 9   How the Organization Contributes to Police Stress and Burnout

Postscript   The Police Burnout Syndrome

"Burnout is a reality, and those in public service are more aware than ever of the danger of being consumed by the very system they are sworn to serve and protect. My deepest hope is that if, by heeding the danger signs of burnout, the reader is able to facilitate a restoration of balance within himself, a peer or a loved one, then my circle has become complete and the goal which I set out to accomplish many years ago has been met."
—Dr. Gerald Loren Fishkin, 1988

PARKHURST
BROTHERS
PUBLISHERS

To Order: 800-621-2736   •   www.parkhurstbrothers.com   •   All major distributors

Psychology / Firefighter and Paramedic

Dealing Effectively with Firefighter Stress

Firefighter and Paramedic Burnout was the first comprehensive book dealing with the recognition and treatment of burnout among firefighter and paramedic personnel. Today, this standard still serves to provide readers with a system of identification of early warning signs of excessive stress, its personal and social consequences, and interventions that have been proven to assist firefighters and their family members to return to a state of health and productivity.

Paperback • $17.95 • 978-1-62491-077-7
215 Pages @ 5" x 8"

Previously Published by Harcourt Brace
Jovanovich Legal and Professional
Publications, Inc.

Now available through
Parkhurst Brothers Publishers.

2016 Author Tour
Radio Promotion

Table of Contents

"This book is for the firefighter/paramedic under stress, and for his family members and peers. Administrators will gain a clearer perspective regarding symptoms of stress among subordinates as well as organizational factors which contribute to or exacerbate employee stress. Finally, therapists will benefit from an understanding of the firefighter's/paramedic's unusual work environment, its effect upon them and their families."
—Dr. Gerald Loren Fishkin, 1989

PARKHURST BROTHERS PUBLISHERS

To Order: 800-621-2736   •   www.parkhurstbrothers.com   •   All major distributors